How to Earn
$15 to $50 an Hour
and more
With a Pickup Truck
or Van

DON LILLY

REVISED EDITION

DARIAN·BOOKS

Glendale, Arizona

Single copy orders available for $12.95 plus $1.00 postage and handling. Address all retail and wholesale inquiries to the PUBLISHER:

DARIAN·BOOKS

P.O. Box 3091
Glendale, AZ 85311

Copyright © 1982 & 1987 by Don Lilly
    1st Printing 1983
    2nd Printing 1987 COMPLETELY REVISED

Library of Congress Cataloging in Publication Data
    Lilly, Don
        How To Earn $15 To $50 An Hour &
        More With A Pick-Up Truck Or Van
    1. Self-employed
    2. Trucking
    3. Junk Trade
    I. Title II. Title: How to earn fifteen
        dollars to fifty dollars an hour and
        more with a pick-up truck or van.
HD8036.L54   1987   388.3'243   86-71695

ISBN 0-910899-09-6 (pbk.)

ABOUT THE AUTHOR

Don Lilly has been self-employed most of his adult life, working as a theatrical and portrait photographer, carpenter, decorator, custom builder, hauler, and now devotes all his time to writing and self-publishing. He spent eight years working with his pick-up before deciding to put it down in writing. He has travelled throughout the United States, Canada, Europe, the Middle East, the Far East and Central America.

Living by his natural talents and adapting them to the locale, he states that unemployment is not based on an outside source or individual. He sees all men as self-employed, all their lives, and that each man has an inherent purpose, place, value, and function. The hauling business is an example of translating this understanding into a simple, workable form. Don told so many people how he stayed employed using his pickup truck when others were claiming there was no work, that he decided to publish this part of his story.

ACKNOWLEDGMENT

I am deeply grateful to the following people for their contributions to this and the first edition.

Lowell Moss of Lowell Moss Creative Services in San Francisco was the cornerstone of my self-publishing career. He volunteered help far and above the call of duty. Maggie Sullivan of Princeton, New Jersey catapulted a disjointed hand-written version to an exciting manuscript form. Dan Poynter of Santa Barbara, CA added all the mechanics of production to this edition. Hank Richter of Phoenix, Arizona provided quips, quotes, valuable comments, and artistic talents.

And I owe a special thanks to Shirley M. of Saugerties, N.Y. for spiritual support beyond measure.

And to Earl Scott who saw the apple fall long before it was ripe. Thank-you all.

Cover Design by Hank Richter

Illustrations by Hank Richter & Don Lilly

CONTENTS

"It's one thing to be moved by world events, but it's so much easier and faster to use a pick-up truck."

1 . . . & MORE

A man calls. He says he just got divorced and he has one load of "junk" to haul away from the house he is vacating. He wants me to do the job that afternoon and he agrees to pay my asking price of $35 per load.

The load of "junk" turns out to be a 6' artificial Christmas tree with all the lights and trimming, numerous electronic games and models left by his son who didn't want them anymore, a library of current best sellers. And bedspreads, blankets, pillows, dinnerware, dishes, lamps, plant hangers and miscellaneous other items, and everything is practically new. Nothing is broken.

He says he's so glad the job could be done so quickly. He's leaving for Florida the next day and is relieved to see everything go. It took an hour and a half to get this load to my home along with the $35 fee.

Does this sound extraordinary? It's not. Six years in the hauling business proved to me our society is so glutted with goods people like this man are anxious to pay $15 an hour to have them taken away.

This example is just one of hundreds of fascinating jobs a man or woman with a pick-up or van can expect to be called to do when he or she knows where and how to ask for such work.

Hauling is an age-old occupation carried on in every country on earth. Whether on the back of a mule, a camel, or a man, in a cart or a pick-up truck or van, the transportation of goods is a necesssity in every community.

Keeping this in mind, if you use the simple technique provided in this book to set your basic prices, you can carry your earning capacity with you wherever you go.

A hauling service can be started in any city, town, or village, in any season, and at any time convenient to you. You set the pace, accept or reject the work as you see fit, and have the freedom and flexibility to do more important activities.

Whether you are an independent contractor with some extra time on hand, a high school student, an unemployed or under-employed worker looking for extra income, or a group such as a Boy Scout troop or Boys Club in need of cash for a special event, you'll find hauling to be both rewarding and satisfying work.

Whether you own a home or are just starting out, if you follow the suggestions outlined, you can just about furnish yourself with everything needed beyond food and housing free of charge and taxes. And if you are diligent and follow through with a recycling program, you can even pay for food and rent through resales.

When I placed my first ad for hauling work, it was a simple translation of my desire to lend a hand. Very soon the rewards beyond my fee began to prove the correctness of my motivation. I was paid to accept the very goods for which I thought I was laboring. And the goods were not always broken, torn, worn-out, or ragged cast-offs. Some were still in their original wrappings. But most were items which simply no longer fit the decor, or the times, or the owner's fancy.

And the best, the few real treasures placed in my care by those too ignorant to recognize 'gold', were handed over as though they were trash. And along with the treasures came a good wage, and a word of gratitude and thanks.

Truthfuly, did you ever think someone would actually pay you to accept such things as a late 19th century oil painting, a new hand-made leather purse retailing at $125, a leather coat with a fur collar, a pair of ski boots used only one season, ladies wool suits in the latest style, valued at well over $100 and never worn, or auto parts, building materials, furniture, toys, carpeting, or stereo equipment?

It's true. And I was paid $15 an hour to haul the items mentioned to the local dump (or wherever I desired). I was even given more, too plentiful to recount.

The most memorable, of course, is the oil painting, which after being cleaned by a professional restorer, is worth about $400. Along with the painting, I was given by the same client a pair of antique kitchen chairs, a single bed frame with mattress and box springs, a stereo amplifier and speakers and a $70 fee for transporting two loads of personal effects - a job which took four hours to complete. The painting and the other items were considered 'junk' and were to be thrown in the dump.

It is common to be given clothes, books, tools, lumber, large and small appliances, kitchen utensils and dishes, and a variety of sporting goods. And it is not uncommon to receive items such as vases, plant stands, picture frames (sometimes with old photographs and prints), rugs, bedding, pet cages, fish tanks, wall hangings,

Christmas tree lights and ornaments, electrical and plumbing supplies, leftover paints, paint rollers, brushes, pans and miscellaneous cleaning materials.

To correct any thought that what I collected was due to my location, most of the jobs I refer to were in and around a town of less than 10,000 population with a high unemployment problem. Throwing away items of value is not a phenomenon related to wealthy areas only. It is common to all classes of income. It is you, the hauler, who must recognize the treasure. The chapter on RECYCLING introduces you to this talent.

There are many opportunities beyond hauling which quickly come to the surface. And this book gives you the step by step plan of action which begins with the hauling service and branches out to include bigger and better opportunities. Some of these possibilities are outlined in the chapter on RELATED JOB IDEAS.

The hauling rates quoted will vary with time, place and circumstance, but no matter when you place your first ad, if you follow the simple rule of making a few calls to others in the same business and asking for their present rates, you'll have a basis for developing your own rate schedule if you choose not to use the schedule included in the chapter on QUOTING. With each job an instinctive quoting ability will begin to grow.

One important **note of caution:** Never, and

I repeat never, offer to haul for no fee, thinking the load will eventually pay for itself. It may or may not. You can't tell until you see it and that brings up the next caution. Never offer to look at the materials to be hauled or moved first and then make a bid. Just stick to the all important rule of making a quote by phone using the RATE SCHEDULE. Otherwise you'll be running all over town making bids and hoping loads will pay for themselves.

Believe me, you will get all the business you want without leaving your desk. I never made a quote on-sight and really never had anyone ask me to. If you expect to make the minimum of $15 an hour in this business, follow this caution I've given you and let the customer decide if it's worth it.

Finally, to prove that an idea works on the practical level, it should work for anyone, as well as it's originator. My brother is an example of a young man who claimed there was no work unless some established business was hiring. And usually they weren't, or they were paying too little to meet his daily needs. Thus he was 'unemployed' quite often.

So I loaned him the money to buy a pick-up and an answering device. He then placed an ad in the local paper just below mine. One of his first jobs was to clear a man's property of leaves and brush. Then the man asked if this brother was available to do some interior painting. He began in the living room. Then he was asked to paint the dining room, hallway, kitchen, the bath, two bedrooms, and finally the entire exterior of the house.

In the meantime, the same man wanted his kitchen floor replaced. I got the contract to install quarry tile. A friend of this man then asked who cleared his property and my brother soon had work from that source. Do you get the point?

My brother no longer claims there is no work, as he knows how to create it on his own. In fact, in the warm months he soon realized he had to turn away some jobs, because he found himself working seven days a week.

I won't claim you will make a million with a pick-up or van - though you might - I simply state, if you need a little water to prime the pump, a little gasoline to fire the engine, then read on, pour away, and watch the water begin to flow, listen to that engine kick over. And forget about 'unemployment'. There's no such condition.

One last note: If you accept the image of a hauling business as dirty work, based on what you've seen of 'trash collectors' in the past, you would be right about 25% of the time. It can be dirty. So what! At $15 an hour and more, who cares. And besides, dust and dirt cannot touch the heart, they cannot penetrate the soul, which is the true man. And too, nothing beats working for yourself. Thus said --

HAPPY HAULING

"One tool - a pick-up truck or van - will get you into business. The other tools will fall into place."

2 EQUIPMENT

Gearing up for a hauling business costs very little since you probably already have most of the basic tools.

Basic Tools

*   Workmens gloves

*   Rope - about 50 feet of strong nylon

*   2 screwdrivers - one regular and one Phillips head type

*   Hammer

*   Pliers with wire cutting feature

*   2 Crescent wrenches

* Scissors

* Pocket knife

* Duct tape

* Five-pronged pitch fork

* Shovel

* Leaf rake

* 2 - 6mil polyethelene tarps

* Old blankets

* Hydraulic jack

* Foot-operated air pump

* 2 well-seasoned 8 foot planks

* Large magnet

Anything on the list which you have to buy, get second hand at a surplus outlet, flea market, or garage sale. You don't need new equipment. Every tool you buy is tax deductible.

TARPS. The tarps are for use in bad weather. Get a roll of 12'x100' - 6 mil vapor barrier used in the building industry at any building supply center. Cut one piece about 30'x12' and another about 12'x8'. Use the leftover roll for your garden or as painting drop cloths.

When you need to use the larger of your cut pieces, lay it down the length of the truck bed starting at the rear and put the excess up on the cab while you load the truck.   When your load is on, simply pull the excess back over the load and secure it at the rear by setting heavy items on it and stuffing the sides down under boxes and other heavy objects.   The smaller tarp is for use when it is drizzling and is used as a temporary cover when loading. It's further use is explained in the chapter on HAULING.

I also have a large heavy canvas tarp with 2' lengths of rope tied to its corners and at intervals along the sides which I tie to the hooks on the truck rack.   This tarp is for long distance furniture hauling. You might find one at a surplus outlet, or look around for a trucker who is getting rid of a used one.   It cannot be stressed enough that securing the tarps will be your most important last step before beginning to drive away.   If there are any loose ends, the wind will work the tarp loose and you will have to stop and do the job right.

BLANKETS.   The old blankets are for padding furniture.   Most of the time I use the customers blankets and carpets.

HYDRAULIC JACK & FOOT-OPERATED AIR PUMP. Carry along the jack and pump for emergencies, and always check your tire pressure on the way to a job, especially if it is going to be a heavy load.   I learned this lesson the hard way.

On one of my first jobs a bucket loader at a gravel pit dumped a load of gravel into my truck bed. When the loader pulled away, I found my rear tires were almost flat. Fortunately, I was within a block of a service station, or I would have had to hand shovel the load off and go for air.

If you do the same thing, or find yourself in a similar situation, place the hydraulic axle jack (a 2 to 4 ton capacity type) under the axle and take the pressure off the tires while you pump in more air.

Learn to judge how much weight you can handle and when someone else is loading you, be certain to direct them as to when to stop. Experience has taught me to pass up gravel hauling jobs with a half-ton pickup because the work involved unloading and the stress on the vehicle are not worth what people will pay for the load. Unless you are equipped with a dumping bed, its better to let men with dump trucks have these jobs.

PLANKS. The 8' planks are for jobs moving pianos or other large items you can't load with a hand truck. Use them as ramps. Don't use green or knotty planks as they'll snap under the weight of a piano. Try to find a few which will bear lots of weight. Go to a used lumber dealer. Look in the yellow pages or ask at your lumber yard. Tell the dealer what you are using the planks for. If all else fails, call a building wrecker and ask if he can supply them.

LARGE MAGNET. Use this to pick up nails and metal objects after you clean up a pile of construction debris or have torn down a shed or outbuilding. Use your imagination with the magnet as many good screws, bolts, nuts, nails, and hardware are lost because they seem to be too small to be worth recovering.

For a complete line of magnets of every kind call or write to: Magnet Sales & Mfg. Co., 11250 Playa Court, Culver City, CA 90230. In California call (213)391-7213. Nationwide call 1-800-421-6692. Ask for their catalog.

Special Tools

HAND TRUCK. I didn't include a hand truck on the essentials list because you can do without one at first, but it is definitely the first non-essential tool in which you should invest. Find a heavy-duty appliance hand truck, like those U-Haul rents, with the rolling skids on the rear for going up and down stairs. These trucks also have a strap which is tightened with a handle device. You might try buying a used one for under $100 from a tool equipment rental shop. The investment is tax deductible and will pay for itself over and over again.

Before I got one my father and I took a job moving a washer and dryer up seven steps. When we got the washer loaded we swore we'd never move appliances again. When we got the hand truck we moved a huge refrigerator and I could do most of the work alone. I needed the extra hand to steer me down the stairs and to hoist the refrigerator onto the truck bed.

Use the hand truck to stack 5 and 6 packed boxes of goods at a time for moving from the house to the truck and vice versa. You can move a lot of boxes, especially ones full of books or records, even if all you have is a cheap small dolley from the hardware store.

You might inquire about the new hand trucks which are built like mini-hydraulic lift trucks. They lift a load so it can be unloaded from a height.

PIANO BOARD. This is a 6' to 8' long 2x8 which is covered on one side with carpeting. Make the board yourself. Use it under a piano or long heavy cabinet. Once its under, slide a few 4-wheel dolleys under the board for moving the object to and from the truck.

4-WHEEL DOLLEY. This is the small platform shape with wheels which move in every direction used by professional movers. They move large heavy bulk items like cabinets, freezers, dressers, or residential liquor bars. The dolley can also be used for pianos.

LIFT GATE. If you get enough calls to move furniture and large appliances to justify adding an hydraulic lift gate to your truck, they can be bought for around $1000 brand new. First though, try truck salvage yards, surplus outlets, or advertise for a used one in the newspaper.

DUMP TRUCK CONVERSION. As your business progresses you might consider converting your pick-up to a dump truck. You can have this done by firms specializing in this business. Or you can build a dumping unit out of wood for between $85 and $100 worth of materials. An order form for this unit is in the back of this book along with a description and photos.

TRAILER HITCH & SIDE MIRRORS. Sometimes you'll need the capacity of two beds for jobs. Put on a trailer hitch and mount side mirrors on you truck or van to see beyond the trailer you've either rented or bought for large jobs. If you own a station wagon and mount a trailer hitch to it you can even run a hauling business without owning a pick-up truck.

PHONE ANSWERING DEVICE. No matter how you feel about answering devices, they work. If you have a regular job and you want to haul on the weekends or in the evening, put on the answering device so callers for your ad can leave a number for you to get back to them when you arrive in the evening. You should be able to get a fairly good one for about $120.00

SNOW PLOW. If you live in an area with moderate to heavy snowfalls, snow plowing is a natural extension of your business - especially if you have a four-wheel drive vehicle. Place a short ad in the classifieds and build a steady customer list.

There's more about snow-plowing in the chapter on RELATED JOB IDEAS.

PICK-UP RACK.   The next step to consider is constructing a simple rack to increase your load capacity.   You can't ask the prices I'm quoting on the RATE SCHEDULE in this book without this extra load capacity.

Build the rack with 6 - 2x4's or metal L's to fit into the bed sides as uprights. There are holes to accomodate these uprights in most models. Frame the tops of the uprights together with 2 - 2x4 siderails and 1 - 2x4 frontrail.   Or if you are using metal L's use them for the sides and front.

Then mount 4 - 1x6 boards to the uprights, 2 to each side at equal intervals between the top of the bed and the bottom of the 2x4 siderail.   You can do the same at the front but the cab can be used as a barrier unless you have a very new vehicle and want to protect it.   Bolt everything together with carriage bolts, nuts and lock washers, and for the 1x6 boards use 2" woodscrews.   If you want a good solid rack, you can have a welder join your metal frame together.   Finally mount hooks on the uprights about 1/4 and 3/4 of the way down each one for tying ropes to them and for securing tarps.   If you don't want to be constantly remembering to bring your ropes, mount them in loops of about 15' lengths to the sides of the rack on hooks. That way they only have to be untied and thrown across a load and tied.

Here are some illustrations for preparing ropes and tying knots.

Whipping

Start the whipping as shown in Fig. 1. Make about four or five turns, pulling each turn as tightly as possible. Lift the end B. in Fig. 1, make several more turns (Fig. 2). Lay the other end of binding string (E) as shown in Fig. 3 and continue to wind over it for four or five more turns. Pull the end E until the loop is drawn under and both ends look alike (Fig. 4). Cut off the ends E and B. If properly whipped, quite a little strength will be needed to pull end E through.

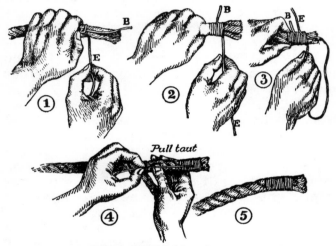

Knots Used for Making Permanent Loops

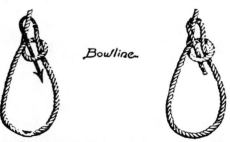

Bowline

A very important knot. Forms a loop that will not slip. Used for several life saving purposes, as well as for fastening horse or boat to a post.

Knots Used for Tying Rope to an Object

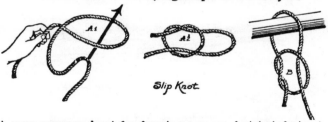

Slip Knot.

A very common knot for forming a noose, but is inferior to two half hitches.

Half Hitch.   Two Half Hitches.   Timber Hitch

Used for tying rope to poles and posts or as a form of slip knot.   Used for hauling logs.

Clove Hitch.   Clove Hitch over bar.

The clove hitch is the most used of all hitches, it being very easy to tie and not apt to slip.

Hitching Tie.

Used for tying halter ropes to a post or a ring.

Knots Used for Shortening the Rope

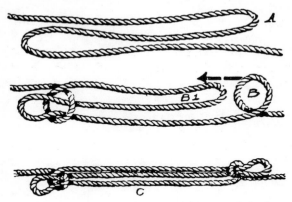

Sheepshank.

Used for shortening a rope. Holds only as long as there is a strain on it.

Knots for Tying Two Ropes Together

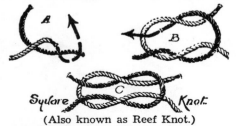

Square Knot.

(Also known as Reef Knot.)

The commonest knot for two ropes of even thickness. Should be used in all First Aid bandaging. Seldom slips or jams unless it catches on an object and fouls.

Sheet Bend.

Used for tying together two ropes of equal or different thickness.

DO NOT build your rack higher than 30"
above the top of the truck bed railing.
30" is sufficient for most jobs and you
won't have to worry about low clearances
in parking garages and other low places.
I built my first rack 36" high and two
days later cracked it off at the bed railing when I drove into a parking garage.

You'll learn with experience to improvise
larger load capacities with the materials
you are hauling. Pick out any panelling
or boards which you can stand higher than
your rack, and set the boards or panelling
along the siderails. Now you can pile a
load as high as the panelling or length of
the boards. Again, watch your clearances
under bridges and crossovers.

The cost of these materials is tax deductible.

The following is an illustration of the
rack.

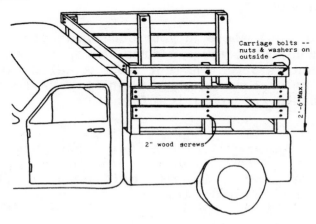

"Opportunity and responsibility go hand in hand."

3 LEGAL MATTERS

To begin your business in a responsible way you must consider these few small legal matters.

Permits

Find out where in your community you can dump, what you can dump there, and what kind of permit is required. A call to the city or town clerk explaining your needs should get you this information.

If the permit is for local residents to dump personal debris, it will be inexpensive, and is usually paid on a yearly basis. Two dollars per year was my last fee and the number of visits was limited to a few times each week. Buy one of these residential permits to begin your business. If dumping does not become a part of your business, you will fall within the usage limit. A permit for dumping the collection from a daily garbage pickup service will naturally cost more, but as mentioned earlier, the book is not about such a service.

Dumping Fees

Some communities without landfills charge on a per/load basis for dumping. The first town I hauled in charged $7/load and no scavenging was allowed. In this case, a per/load charge would have to be added to the hauling charge and you can't expect much profit. So find other ways to get rid of stuff you'd normally take to the dump.

For example, a relative or friend may need some landfill on their property and would allow you to dump brush, stone, leaves, and other organic matter, except household garbage. If you have a big problem getting rid of such refuse, shift your focus through the wording of your classified ad to moving furniture, appliances, or general delivery work, or any of the other services discussed in the chapter on RELATED JOB IDEAS.

Licenses

Call your town or city clerk and find out

about their licensing procedures. A license is sometimes needed to move items for households other than your own and relatives and friends. At first, you can consider any job as that of a friend or relative until you can afford a license. The license filing fee is not prohibitive and in the state of New Jersey is a one-time-only affair. You pay $150 a year and renew the license yearly without cost.

Once you start advertising and moving a lot of households, you'll want to be above board and have that license. A few loads hauled and the license will be paid for. Since trucking is now deregulated, such licenses may not be required.

One final note of interest: I wondered if running a small moving business as suggested in this book was upsetting to the larger van lines which pay substantial licensing fees to do business. On discussing the matter with the owner of a large Phoenix, Arizona based firm, I was told the small independent movers were performing a service for the community which his firm could not provide. The cost of moving a piano, for example, one mile down the road was prohibitive for his firm and thus the independent mover with a pick-up truck was actually filling the void.

Insurance

You need liability protection in case something you are moving gets damaged and the customer wants you to repair or replace it. In the beginning, don't spoil your enthusiasm for getting into this business because you think there is too much expense and red tape to get yourself off the ground. I learned as I went along. I was extra careful not to drop things and to tie everything down securely and I thus never had a problem with breakage. Besides, you can deduct the expense of repair or you can repair things yourself.

Allow nothing to stop you from earning a living. Just do your best and every problem will work itself out. If you feel you want insurance coverage, call your agent and ask about a rider which can be added to your truck policy to cover goods you haul every now and then for other people. Don't make it sound as though you're in the big time hauling and moving business. In fact, play the whole business down, as agents will try to sell you the world, given the chance. If you can't afford insurance right away, get some loads under your belt and consider it when you feel you can afford it.

One other kind of insurance you should consider, if you rent your place of residence; tenants' insurance. I found out the hard way that auto policies do not cover theft of tools and equipment from the vehicle. Ask your agent if your tools are covered on any of your present policies. Ask to be shown where the coverage is stated. If its not there, get it.

"Doing business without advertising is like winking at a girl in the dark."

4 ADVERTISING

Promotion is the key to any successful venture. Potential customers must know you are available and what you have to offer before they will call on you.

Ad Placement

Place an ad in the service column of your local newspaper. You need not place it every day if your paper is a daily; two or three times a week is plenty. If your paper is a weekly, place the ad each week. Keep accurate records of your advertising costs because they are deductible as business expenses.

At first, take all jobs as they come,

perform them courteously at the time agreed upon, and soon your business will be off and running. Sometimes you may have so much business you may have to take the ad out for a few times. Don't advertise for customers you do not have time to service. That will discourage those people from trying you another time. On the other hand, don't ruin your reputation for reliability by taking on more work than you can handle.

Be consistent in advertising. Once you choose and place an ad, stick with the same wording regardless of the temptation to improve and revise. A stable ad gives you the image of a stable and reliable person. Regular users of the classifieds will notice your ad even when they aren't looking for a hauler.

If you want to add a certain feature to your range of services, by all means include it - but at the end of your ad. Your headline should not change.

Ad Sample

A simple, direct ad will be the most effective. Use this one to start your business.

NEED A PICK-UP(VAN) for a small or medium-sized load? Moving locally? Heavy appliances, brush piles, construction debris, junk. Whatever your hauling needs. Call Don. 555-1212.

In time you might want to develop your own wording to better suit your particular situation and locality. To maintain that rule of consistency, place my ad and take jobs as they come. Then when you have an ad of your own, place it simultaneously with mine for several weeks or months, and then pull mine out and see how yours goes. If it works, fine. Stick with it. If not, just place mine again.

For a van place this ad.

NEED A VAN for a small or medium-sized load? Moving locally? Deliveries made. Specializing in artwork and sculptures. Whatever. Call Don. 555-1212

Notice I shifted the focus from possible calls with brush, construction materials, etc., to items suited to a van, especially deliveries and even art work. This service is talked about in detail in a later chapter.

Additional Promotion

You can get free advertising by placing an ad on super market and laundromat and college bulletin boards. You can insert ads under car windshield wipers at shopping centers, or wherever you shop. Make it a habit to carry ads with you and place them often and profusely.

Here's an inexpensive way to make these ads. Divide an 8-1/2 x 11 piece of paper into eight equal sections by drawing a line down the center and 3 horizontal lines at equal intervals down the page. Then clearly print or type your ad on each block. This one page serves as your master copy to run off 8 ads for the price of one at a copy center. You only need to cut them apart and you have a good supply. Take the sample master from the back of the book and have the clerk at the copy center read this paragraph and then ask her to help you construct your sheet.

Also consider a simple magnetic sign for each of your vehicle doors. You can, of course, remove the signs whenever you want to use your truck or van for private trips.

In time, have a business card printed to leave with customers for future reference and to pass your phone number on to friends. Take the sample cards provided in the back of the book to your copy center or printer and choose the card you like for duplication with your name, address, and phone number on it. Or you may want to have your printer help you lay out a simple card showing all the features of your particular service. For example, all of these may be included on one card; hauling, rototilling, snow-plowing, firewood.

There are many people you can approach more directly for business. Real estate agents are often faced with managing or trying to sell a property with a cluttered or debris-strewn apartment, garage, basement, or yard. They need help clearing out junk and hauling it away. Visit or call local agents and offer your services. Leave a sample of your ad or your business card. Also, ask them to recommend you to their clients who may be moving locally.

Call on local contractors and ask for any cleaning up jobs they can't handle themselves. Offer them 10% of the profit if they recommend you for large jobs on the bigger sites. Make the offer only if it seems absolutely necessary. Many contractors make it a practice to subcontract such work out.

Condominium and Coop managers often need a ready hand. Call on them and leave your ad or card. Keep your calls casual and friendly. Don't be pushy. Establish a friendly relationship with local business people, and in time, they will call.

If you live in a larger town or city, drop your card off with apartment managers and superintendents, and offer them 10% of your profits from jobs for which they recommend you. Don't be tight about sharing your profits in this instance, as one apartment complex can bring you a lot of business. Make sure you pay the commission as promised. Your business will flourish when it is run honestly.

Have pre-gummed labels printed (it's cheaper by the thousand) stating your service, your name, and your phone number. Stick these near mailboxes in large apartment buildings, or in elevators. Get permission from the superintendent first. Locksmiths usually place similar stickers.

In some cities, there are job hotlines for people to call for help. If one is available near you, place your number on file for hauling or whatever service you offer. Then when someone calls in for help, you are in the reference file for consideration. Some volunteer social groups have switchboards set up to provide the community with all kinds of help not available through conventional channels. Place your name and service with these groups.

Let your fellow church members know what services you have available. Contact every social club you can think of, like Kiwanis, Lions, Moose, and let the members know through their newsletters or other media that you are available for hauling and other types of jobs.

Don't forget Women's Clubs, Garden Clubs, and especially Senior Citizen Clubs and organizations. They are a windfall of potential clients, always in need of sincere, good help. Check the yellow pages under Clubs, Associations and Groups.

If you are in or near a university town, there is a constant flow of apartment moving going on. Make sure your ad is on every bulletin board, kiosk, and information center. And be sure to find out what newspaper the students use so you can keep an ad in front of their attention.

One last idea; when you go to auctions, either to buy or to observe, let the auctioneer know you are available to haul so he can make a brief announcement or point you out to anyone needing a hand getting their treasure home. Or simply put a sign on your truck and stand near it until you are approached.

"The only reason worry kills more people than work is that more people worry than work. Place the ad now!"

"Never grow a wishbone where a backbone ought to be."

5 HOW TO QUOTE A JOB

In this age of telemarketing, many sales of goods and services are taken care of by telephone. Your success at getting jobs by phone will depend on your ability to quickly work out a price which will satisfy both you and your potential client.

To make a good quote you should know the load size and its make-up, the distance to the job, and the distance between pick-up and delivery if you are moving household goods.

You should also know the details of the location for example, if their are stairs, and if there will be help available to carry and lift the heavy items.

Taking Calls

It is important to be brief, businesslike, and firm, but friendly. Remember, whoever calls has work for you, so take it for granted the job is already yours unless you decide to reject it for some reason. Have an appointment book and a detailed street map of your area and the surrounding communities beside your phone.

The two most common calls you'll get are for loads to the dump and household moving jobs. Moving jos will range from a single item to whole households. As you gain experience, you get a feeling for the questions to ask to be fair in quoting.

I've included a Basic Rate Schedule to cover any type job you might receive and to make it easy for you to give a quick quote on the phone. Your big advantage here is the high price most moving companies must charge. The people who call you probably cannot afford a moving company and will find someone with a pick-up or van to do the job. Usually, you will be moving women or ederly people who cannot load a U-Haul or similar rental vehicle.

If, after making the quote, the caller feels the price is way out of line, ask him to call a moving company or U-Haul, or another independent mover, and after getting some prices, to call you back if he still needs you.

You can remind the caller too, that your load price includes the price of a chauffeur(yourself) to drive the truck, the muscle you provide, the truck, the gas, the overhead on the truck and equipment, including insurance, and your expertise. All these for $35/load.

Don't be intimidated into reducing your fees, because the prices quoted in this book have been used in a number of areas around the country and have proven to be fair and competitive. The prices may fluctuate to higher rates in the larger cities. Calling other haulers and delivery services in your city will give you ideas on how to set your rates.

You'll find through experience that the clients who don't question your rates will also be the most helpful. On the contrary, those who do resist your prices but finally accept, will resist in other ways and possibly make the job a miserable experience for you.

Sample Phone Quotation

Here is how I handle a typical phone call and get the information I need to make an immediate quote.

Caller: I saw your ad. I'm moving to Main from Broadway. What do you charge for the furnishings in a single bedroom apartment?

Myself: What are our largest and heaviest items?

Caller: I have a double bed with a mattress and box springs, a dresser and mirror, kitchen tables and chairs, a refrigerator, a couch and end tables, and a heavy desk.

(This information indicates a minimum of three loads and that a hand truck will be needed. The caller did not mention boxes of books and miscellaneous items, dishes, wall-hangings and bedding, but these extras must be taken for granted. Bulk items fill the truck or van quickly, but will rarely make four loads from a one bedroom apartment.)

Myself: Are there any stairs at either end and will you or friends be able to help with carrying and lifting?

Caller: There are stairs at the receiving end, but only five, and I have a friend who will help carry and lift.

Myself: Approximately how many miles are there between the two locations.

Caller: About three.

(So, five stairs should not be considered a flight and will not require an extra charge, you will not have to hire help, and since the distance is only three miles no charge is added to cover excessive time and gas usage. (Look at the Rate Chart concerning mileage.)

Myself: My fee is $35 a load and without seeing the goods I'd estimate no more than three loads for a total of $105.00 for the entire job. When do you want me to move you?

(Don't hesitate after you state your fee to ask for an appointment time.)

Caller: Tomorrow, if possible.

Myself: How about 8:30 in the morning?

Caller: That's fine.

(Don't put off work you can do immediately. Decisive action gets you the job. You may lose work to other haulers who are faster on the draw. Begin as early in the morning as possible. The later you start, the less time you have to make adjustments due to unforeseen problems, like flat tires. And you can schedule one-load jobs for later in the day.)

Myself: May I have your name, address, phone number, and instructions on how to get to your home?

(Write these in your appointment book along with your agreed arrival time, approximate number of loads and the quoted price. Write precise directions given to you to the client's home. When taking directions, if the area is unfamiliar to you, lay your map out in front of you and have the client lead you verbally from a point familiar to both or you to his home. As you look at the map, make sure you see your way there mentally from his description.

When taking directions in his neighborhood, write down local landmarks, the side of the street his house is on, the name on the mailbox, the color of the house, etc., so that you will be sure to find him and not waste your day and his by circling aimlessly. Punctuality is important. No one likes to wait, and any excuse other than real emergencies just makes you seem inept.)

Myself: One last point. Is all the packing completed because I charge $7.50 per load additional if I have to wait until the packing is finished?

Caller: I'll have everything ready by the time you get here.

Myself: Good. Then I'll see you at 8:30 in the morning and I'll call if there are any delays. Goodbye.

After you hang up, put the client's name, address, phone number, quoted price, type of job, and pick-up and delivery locations on a 3 x 5 card and put the card in your appointment book in the page you have the written directions. After the job, enter the gross profit on the card, the number of actual loads, and any wages paid out for help. Then file the card for future reference. It will be of great help when determining prices on similar jobs, and it is useful at tax time.

Not all calls will be as involved as this one, and the majority will be simpler, as most jobs will not be for residential moving unless that's what you decide to concentrate on.

When you first start quoting, get all the basic information by writing it quickly on a scrap of paper, and then ask the caller to hold the line while you work up your quote from the Basic Rate Schedule. Get out the schedule and fit together the type of job, special considerations, and then add them up. Make your quote, explaining your basic rate and each additional fee where applicable. Then, ask when you can start the job.

A note regarding the arrangement of furniture: I'm not saying you shouldn't take beds and dressers to the bedroom of the new location, but don't get talked into placing each piece in it's place unless you're told exactly what spot it goes to in the room and if that spot is free.

BASIC RATE SCHEDULE

Job Type	Special Considerations	Basic Rate
Trash, junk, debris, etc.	Within 5 mile radius of your home	$25-$30/load
	Outside 5 mile radius	Add $5/load for every 10 extra miles
	For example:	
	Up to 15 mile radius	$30/load
	Up to 25 mile radius	$35/load
	(The mileage fee varies with the price of gas)	
	For an unpredictable number of loads, such as leaf or brush piles	$20/load plus $5/hr.
Furniture, appliances, & household goods	Within 5 mile radius of your home & no helper	$35/load
	Outside 5 miles radius	Add $5/load for every 10 extra miles
	If 1 flight of stairs	Add $5/load
	If 2 flights or more	Add $10/load

Use these rates only as guidelines to begin your hauling business and remain flexible depending on the job, circumstances, and location. These rates merely help you to get the ball rolling immediately and set the stage for you to eventually work up your own rate schedule.

Job Type	Special Considerations	Basic Rate
	If you hire a helper	Add $15/load
	If client is still packing & holds up loading job	Add $7.50/load
	If you are to help pack	Add $8-$10/hr.
	If you are to arrange furniture at destination	Add $7.50/hr.
Piano moving	Requires 3 extra men & if within 5 mile radius	$40 flat rate plus $10 per extra man
Long distance hauling		$15/hr. plus gas plus tolls or an alternative: $1.25/mile door to door plus tolls (Door of pickup to door of delivery)

RENTING EQUIPMENT

When you rent equipment such as chain saws, plows, roto-tillers, or cutting torches, etc., add the rental cost to your basic fee and don't forget to figure in the mileage to and from the rental shop.

Get as much help from the client as possible, including youngsters, by pointing out to your client your fee is for loading your truck, driving it, and unloading it, preferably to the ground from the back of the tailgate. Point out too, that you are not charging by the hour and thus your time is very valuable and the help of friends makes the job go quickly.

"A persons pick-up truck or van is his own personal portable employment agency."

"Life is like a pick-up truck... It's not much fun driving around empty."

6 MOVING & HAULING

This chapter will be a simple run-through of a furniture moving job, though much of the information is valuable for any hauling job. At the end of the chapter are some general tips. How to sort and load for a dump trip will be described in the chapter on RECYCLING.

Basic Preparation

You're preparing for your first job. Let's say it's an apartment moving job of possibly 3 loads of household items. Though it includes a refrigerator, the client agreed to help move it so you are going alone. About half an hour before your appointment time, call and tell the client you are on your way. This call serves a number of purposes. It confirms your appointment, it alerts the client to finish packing and have everything ready to load, and it reassures him that you will be on time. Moving is a trauma and your disposition and punctuality on moving day is a tremendous morale booster.

If any trouble develops with your vehicle, or some other emergency comes up, be absolutely certain to call and inform your client. Then do everything you can to get there as soon as possible. DON'T cancel out and leave the client high and dry. He's counting on you. Most likely he had to vacate the property that day and may be taking off work to make the move. Not only your reputation, but what is more important, another's peace of mind is at stake.

Do a mental run-through of the job as you picture it might be. In this case your loads will be heavy, so check the tire pressure. Fill up the gas tank on the way and check the water and oil. Put your map and quote card with the directions on the dashboard.

Make sure you have the basic tools such as a screwdriver, gloves, tape, etc., including ropes, old blankets or pads, and tarps. If it looks like rain, make sure you have plastic tarps. If you have a hand truck, take it for the refrigerator.

Loading Instruction

When you arrive, if it is raining at all, lay your large plastic tarp on the bed of the truck as described on the chapter on EQUIPMENT, and cover it temporarily with the smaller tarp. This keeps the bottom of the tarp dry in case cardboard cartons must be set on it. Place the cartons and other items under the temporary tarp until you can begin pulling the main tarp back over it from off the cab of the truck.

If it's a sunny day, lay just the main tarp on the bed of the truck and immediately start loading the mattresses and box springs on their sides or ends along the side of the bed against the rack. Slide the mirrors or paintings between them. The tarps are used in all weather to protect items sitting directly on the truck bed, such as mattresses, etc., and to secure the load from wind and rain which could develop in transit.

Don't pack for the client without reminding him that your packing fee is in addition to the load fee. This fee for packing should be mentioned when the original quote is made. You don't want to pack. It's not fun and you're liable for breakage and missing items, etc. So set the fee so high he's not likely to hire you to do it, but if he does you are more than sufficiently compensated. Most likely he would not have called you to haul for him if he had that kind of money.

The same goes for unpacking. Sure you

should place big items in their proper rooms, but arranging and unpacking should carry a price high enough to be rejected or to make it worth your time.

Next to be loaded are the big bureaus and chests. Remove their drawers and carry them out separately. The drawers should be full. Once you have loaded the bureaus, replace the drawers and tape them shut, using your duct tape. Be sure the bureaus are placed so the drawers open toward the cab of the truck or toward the center of the bed, never to the outside, even when taped.

If you haul a stove, tape the oven door shut after you've packed a few small items in it and tape the elements or grills securely in place. Place fragile items like lamps, shades, pottery, sculpture, smaller paintings, boxes of good china, portable TV's and stereos, etc., up in the cab for safe keeping. Load kitchen chairs on last, upside down, with their backs secured between the rack and the load.

Fill every space available on the truck bed, putting the heavy bulk of the load toward the front of the truck. Pack tightly enough to avoid load movement of any kind, but not so close as to scratch or mar anything. Use the old blankets or pads to keep furniture surfaces from touching each other. This won't be necessary for all pieces of furniture. Consult the client about which pieces are most important to protect, and borrow more old blankets from him if he wants a great many pieces protected.

Don't stretch loads; that is, don't under-load to make two trips when the job can be done in one. The client will catch on and it's not the way to build a good reputation. If you have the time to do twice as much work, schedule two jobs for the same day.

If you don't use a tarp over the load, tie ropes across, around, and through every-thing which might move or become airborne or jar loose. If you have boxes on the top course of the load, make sure their lids are taped shut or the wind will empty them for you.

While driving, take it easy and watch constantly for problems. If possible, have the client drive behind you, but not too close, so you can see him in your rear-view mirror. Instruct him to flash his headlights if trouble develops which you cannot see from the cab.

Unloading is faster than loading, but the same rule applies as for loading. You, as the owner of the truck, should personally place all the items in their final loaded position and you should unload them. This way you're sure it's done correctly. Be-sides, you and you alone are responsible for everything while it is on your truck. Unload items either onto the truck gate or set them on them on the ground.

Let helpers carry them into the house. Always form a chain when there are two or more helpers. It's fast and saves many extra steps per person, especially if there are any flights of stairs. Station a man on each landing and have each one carry items from only one landing to the next.

Getting Paid

Finish up, and when you've closed the gate on the truck, walk into the house and take out your wallet. This is a very effective signal that you want to be paid. To keep it from looking too obvious and pushy, have one of your cards or advertisement slips in the dollar bill section. Get it out and hand it over, mentioning that you do painting or yard work or whatever.

If your wife has shown interest, mention that she is available at $5 or $6 an hour to help clean and arrange things. This is also the time to feel around for other related jobs. But do it in a tactful way and then go. I mention this method of collecting your wage for those who find that aspect of business the most difficult.

If, after a job, there is ever a question about the quoted price, get out your quote card to be certain you are right. No reductions should be given because you are hauling more than one load of furniture. Each load should be moved for the same price.

The only time you might give such a break is on loads to the dump such as leaves or brush which are sometimes impossible to estimate in number. People are more reluctant to pay to get rid of something as trash than they are to have something moved. If you can talk someone into a three-load leaf job by reducing your rate to $20 per load, go ahead and do it. But add $5 per hour to cover the reduction in load fee. It could take all day · just to get 3 loads of grass and brush onto the truck and to the dump if the loading is in a difficult position.

General Tips

* Carry extra cash, maybe $30 or $40 with you in case of emergencies.

* Do not run a one-man-show on furniture and appliance jobs. You can't do it. Always ask for all the help the client can round up, including youngsters for the lighter items and to form chains to get the small items into the house quickly. You not only save time looking for extra help but you avoid having to charge a higher fee.

* Take care to instruct the youngsters to be careful when they help out and don't let them lift heavy pieces.

* Always look for ways to improve your loading system to save time and energy on any job you are doing. Smoother, more efficient loading methods improve your profits by giving you more time for more jobs in the same day.

* If you must lay a refrigerator down, check first with a dealer about the brand you are moving. Most can be layed down for a short period, but some cannot be.

* Pack spaces inside appliances, such as the clothes dryer, wash machine, or refrigerator with pillows, stuffed toys, and light weight goods.

* If possible, for good tables, lay them on their tops, legs up, making sure to protect the finish with padding. Many tables legs are removable. Check this and remove them to make an easier job.

* Ask if anything you are hauling has flammable substances in them, like a lawn mower. If so, empty it out first. If you must transport flammables, make certain the lids are secure and no spillage can occur. It would be better if you asked that such flammables be left behind or transported in some other way.

* For any type of job, use your imagination when faced with apparently complex problems. Survey the problem, tell the prospective customer you will get back to him tomorrow, and go home and think about the solution. The bigger the job, and the tougher it is, the more you should charge to do it. It is expected that special problems will cost more to correct.

Here is one example: A man wanted a cast-iron furnace removed from his basement. Four previous haulers had refused the job. They could not work out how to get that enormous weight and size up the cellar steps. I said I'd think about it and would call in the morning.

I knew he was willing to pay well because he had so many refusals. So I let my imagination wonder, not letting price limit my thinking. Finally, I realized the furnace had been carried to the basement in pieces and constructed there. I inquired about the price for renting a cutting torch, hired a young welding student to cut the furnace apart and we carried it out in four pieces. I charged $100 for the job. I paid $25 for torch rental, $15 to the helper, and I got $20 for the scrap metal. It took four hours to complete the job, so I had $20 per hour for my efforts.

Piano Moving

Piano moving requires a minimum of four men. This is for studio and upright models only. You can't move baby and grand pianos. You'd be smart to pass up moving pianos if more than two stairs are involved. Let such jobs go to the pros who have the proper equipment and the know-how. A few stairs would be no problem. But don't forget to take a few well-seasoned planks for sliding the piano down the steps and to get it onto the bed of the truck. Tie the piano to the rack of the truck and have a few of your men ride with it to steady it and keep it from rolling around. And remind the men to be extra careful to hold on so they don't

lose their balance when and if the piano
should roll or shift it's weight.

Suggested Reading

U-Haul Moving Guide. It's free and available at or through your local U-Haul
dealer. It's very informative.

"If you own a pick-up truck or van, you'll
never again hear yourself say, 'I can't
find any work.'"

"Unemployment is not a fact, but a curable incorrect state of mind. And this book proves that statement if you own a pick-up or van and are unemployed."

7 HIRING HELP

Hire a man only when you cannot do the work alone and the client cannot find help. Keeping your prices competitive and avoiding as much as possible the question of workman's compensation are just two reasons to do it alone.

Trash, debris, and junk loads rarely require extra help. If there is just one heavy item, talk your client into helping you get it onto the truck. Getting it off is not so much of a problem. Hiring a man to go along for one or two heavy pieces is just not cost effective. Of course, if you have so much business that time becomes a real factor, then take on a second man and accept twice as much work.

Mention when hiring your men that they are responsible for their own taxes and that you will not be held responsible for injuries sustained while they are working with you. To further protect yourself, you should run off a copy of the sample Release of Liability form which you will find in the Appendix at the back of the book. Get it signed and dated by each helper before you take him/her on the job. Keep the form on file for future reference and for any questions the IRS may have for you when and if an audit of your taxes may arise.

Sources for Help

Ask members of your family, friends, high school job office, the local Community College job office, or drop in at a local barbell club and find an ample supply of muscle.

Helpers' Wages

Which method to use when paying your help is a matter of preference. You can offer an hourly rate. I pay between $4.50 and $7.50 depending on the job and the initiative of the helper.

Be sure to make it clear the clock does not start ticking until the work begins and when it ends. Travel to and from the job should not be charged to you. Of course, the time from the site to the dump is part of the job. I'm referring strictly to before and after the job. If you have a breakdown, you'd better clarify your position right away. You cannot pay for the time it takes to repair the vehicle.

You can also offer a percentage of the gross profit. 35% is a fair amount. If you are questioned about the split, as you might be by a close friend or family member, explain the costs you have already incurred in advertising, time to quote and prepare for the job, vehicle and equipment expenses.

You can offer a flat fee per load also. This is probably the easiest form of payment as you simply add it to your basic load fee when you make the quote and you have no unforeseen losses or arguments about splits or time to and from the job. Be sure to keep accurate records of the wages paid your help as they are deductible as subcontractor's wages.

You will develop your own personal technique for handling quotes and dealing with helpers. Seek fairness for all and you cannot fail.

"Hauling - the longest running road show in history."

"Without realizing it, people are hiring you for $15 an hour and more, to take away, tax free, products and merchandise, and valuable unrecognized treasures."

8 RECYCLING

The real profit in hauling lies in recycling. If you can find uses or markets for items other people pay you to take away, you can increase your profit to hundreds of dollars for just one load of "junk".

How To Classify "Junk"

Begin to think about recycling possibilities as you load. When you arrive on the site, back in close to the pile you are to haul away and start pitching. Make it a habit to ask people to put their junk into one area. Don't clean properties if you quote by the load. Add $5 per hour to your load price if the debris you are to haul away is strewn all around and you have to collect it.

As you load, separate out only the truly valuable and breakable items. Set them aside and pitch everything else onto the truck. Then put the good things on the top of the load or up front in the cab with you. When you get to the dump, take the good things off the top of the load and set them aside again. Then start a breakdown of the remaining load.

Sift through all bags and boxes, as people often throw junk into boxes of perfectly good items and then mistakenly dump all of it at once. Set aside anything you can use, sell, repair, trade, or donate. Dump the rest. Reload all that you set aside to recycle, like good wood, metal, auto batteries, etc. You will eventually classify each item into one of these categories:

* things you can use yourself

* things you can sell immediately

* things you can repair and sell

* things you can trade

* things you can donate

* things you can sell as scrap

* things you should throw in the dump

You'll be taking a lot of stuff home.

Some of it you will be able to use in your own household or workshop, but most of it you won't. Therefore, you're going to have to get rid of it quickly. Don't hoard it, which can happen unintentionally. Only a few truckloads of goods will fill a single car garage. Don't allow a build-up of unneeded items.

The more you hoard the less you will earn. Not only will some things rust, rot, and corrode, but eventually your family or neighbors are going to demand you clean up the junkyard you're creating. The pressure will cause you to think of quick and easy ways to get rid of it. Then you will be in the same position as the person for whom you hauled the goods in the first place. You will either deal off the entire lot for disaster prices, or dump it, and thus lose even more in the labor of a second hauling job - this time for no pay.

So, a word to the wise - don't hoard. Classify after each load and get to work immediately making room for the next load which means placing ads, fixing, trading, donating, etc. Moving inventory is the key to big profits in recycling.

Things You Can Use

First take out items you can use when you first start into a pile of debris. If you come across something you already have, but the one on your load is better than yours, keep the best and sell, trade, or give yours away. Watch for gifts for

Christmas or for birthdays. You'll be surprised how often you'll be given new, never-been-opened items.

I keep all tools and building materials for my home workshop and small contracting business. You'll be given all kinds of hardware supplies, so, if you're patient and thrifty, and organized, you'll sort and store. At the rate the price of these hardware goods has been increasing, the time you put into sorting and storing is worth it.

If you're not a contractor or a do-it-yourselfer, you can still cash in on all the plumbing, electrical, and building supplies which come your way. Keep five gallon buckets handy in your garage or storage area so you can throw each kind of part into them. Put plumbing parts into one, electrical into another, and whatever other categories of goods you develop and sell the buckets at one price to independent plumbers or electricians. A plumber may be willing to pay you $10 for a bucket of various fixture parts. That's $10 above what you were paid in the first place.

Things You Can Sell Immediately

Your biggest profits will come from sales in the Bargain Mart section of the classifieds for the items of obvious value after just a little cleaning and repair. Call your newspaper for the maximum number of words for the minimum price and waste no words or space when forming the ad.

If you only have one high priced item like a refrigerator, stove, or couch, construct your ad to include a few smaller priced items so as not to waste advertising money. Run your ad for three days at a time if it's a daily paper. If you sell everything the first day the ad appears, call the paper and cancel the last two days of the ad.

Sample Appliance Ad

Be brief and to the point when writing your ad. For example:

> G.E. HOTPOINT refrigerator. 17 cubic feet, like new. $150. Call Don. 555-1212.

If you never placed an ad, look in the Bargain Mart and copy the style or details of a similar ad to the one you need to place. Or ask the classifieds sales person to help you construct the ad. Always include the price of an item in the ad. Remain firm when asked if you will take less.

Jot down the names and numbers of those who want to buy for less and if you can't find a buyer, consider calling them if the offers are within reason. You'll know if the price you're asking is way out of line because you won't get any calls, or if you find those coming to look are put off enough by the price not even to give you a smaller offer.

If a big item doesn't sell, and you know the price is within reason, wait a month and readvertise it for a little less. Or change your strategy and begin thinking of other ways to sell it.

An incentive you can hold back to the very last when trying to sell a large item is an offer to deliver.

Make it a practice to ask the least for an item so you can get a fast sale. Your object is to sell quickly and avoid an inventory buildup.

Special Markets

REAL ESTATE FIRMS. Another selling strategy to consider is to call local real estate firms which manage rental properties if you have large appliances for sale. Many times they are looking for inexpensive substitutes. Ask the agents for the names of the owners of multiple rental properties and keep them on file for either sales prospects, or for future hauling job offers. Every now and then send them one of your cards or a copy of your ad. Also call managers of apartment complexes, condominiums, and co-ops and tell them what you have for sale.

GARAGE SALES & FLEA MARKETS. Smaller, less profitable pieces can be sold through a weekly or monthly garage sale or flea market. Old photos, postcards, and even old newspapers are becoming collectors items. Approach flea market and antique shop dealers either at the flea market or through the yellow pages and offer them the entire lot. Don't try to get top dollar for everything you sell or you will begin losing money in the extra time invested in going from one buyer to another.

You're still making a profit on the goods twice, no matter what you get because you were paid to accept them in the first place.

SURPLUS OUTLETS. Second-hand stores and surplus outlets buy either singly or in lots. Know what you want to charge before you approach these dealers and don't be bullied into unloading at absurd prices. If you have unfamiliar items and can't price them, ask for an offer. If you're sure you can get more and they won't come to your minimum requirements in price, then walk away.

INDEPENDENT CONTRACTORS. Don't forget the small, independent contractors who need all kinds of construction materials, new and used. A good, old, well-seasoned beam is still a better beam than a new green one. Get to know local carpenters, plumbers, electricians, and builders. Tell them you have building materials for sale.

Call the lumber yards and buildings centers for prices for new items and offer yours for 1/4 to 1/2 less. Have an inventory list with the dimensions or descriptions of your goods handy and list the prices as you receive them. Then when you sell the wood or whatever, you will be prepared with a price for an individual piece or for the entire lot.

FARMERS & ORGANIC GARDENERS. You can try selling or trading composted leaves by the load to organic gardeners or small farmers in exchange for produce, fresh eggs, of fresh milk. I traded a $30 rototilling job for a gallon of fresh milk delivered to my home once a week for 15 weeks.

CONSIGNMENT SHOPS. Consignment shops are good markets. They will sell items for 33% of what they can sell your goods for. It may take a while to see actual cash, but if you get a good flow of items going into the shop, it could mean a regular check in the mail.

AUCTIONS. There are auctions in some cities which sell on consignment. You take your goods in on a certain specified day, and whatever the auctioneer gets for your items is split 50-50. This is a great market for large lots of bric-a-brac and knick-knacks.

BOOK FAIRS & USED BOOK STORES. If you don't want to donate books you receive to your school or local library, you might consider having a book fair at the end of a long season. Or keep a special table for books at your garage sale. They are a highly saleable commodity. Used bookstores buy books as well as magazines.

Special Items

TROPHIES. Of all things, trophies of any sport and occasion are in high demand, even when used. People remove the plates containing the former champion and replace the plates with their own champions name.

PLASTIC FLOWERS. Plastic flowers will sell again and again. A flea marketeer who heard I'd been tossing mine away because I thought they were useless agreed to buy all I could get. Wait until you have a few boxes full and offer them for $5 or $10 a box.

TUBS & TOILETS. Watch for renovation jobs where old plumbing fixtures are being removed. Ask for the tubs and toilets, pipes and fittings. If the toilets are still good, clean them up and sell them for $15 each. If the tubs have lips all the way around, like the old styles often did, offer them to farmers and horse ranchers who need them for watering troughs. They bring around $15 each.

PIANOS. Old pianos of apparently no value can be sold to piano repair shops. Ask the person having the piano hauled away for the make and model if it is available. Then before the hauling job, call a few piano repairmen and tell them what you are about to get. Take whatever you are offered, providing the distance from the pick-up point does not make the trip worth the price you are offered.

Things You Can Repair And Sell

Determine what is worth repairing. You'll get a lot of furniture, toys, appliances, both small and large, and household goods that have been thrown out simply because they are outdated or considered too dirty to clean up. Some are saleable just as you receive them. Most need a good cleaning and some minor repair, or a little paint. Use your discretion when deciding what to repair.

Don't repair anything which will sell for less than $10. It's easier to donate the repairable items of small value to the Salvation Army or some other such charitable organization. They have repairmen working for them who bring slightly damaged goods back into the marketplace through their outlet stores.

If you are living with or near your parents, and your father is retired or unemployed, has the time and inclination, and is handy with tools, see if he'd be interested in repairing some of the things you bring home. You could pay for the repair materials and split the profits after taking out the cost for your materials.

Or you could find a friend or neighbor or someone through a newspaper ad who would be willing to become your all-around repair man. Again, keep in mind, to make repairing worth the time, concentrate on items which you can sell for $10 and more.

Remember, one of the best ways to price your goods is to call or visit a dealer with the same or similar item for sale, get his price and then cut yours in half. Visit flea markets and antique shops to learn the prices of antiques and semi-antiques. And there are many good reference books on collectibles.

Always keep in mind that you set your prices for a quick turn-over, unless you have a large storage area or shop, or you decide to deal out your goods through a flea market, garage sale, or a consignment shop. Even then you should offer irresistible prices because it is a second profit.

LARGE & SMALL APPLIANCES. Refrigerators are good examples of what I would consider for repair, especially if they are relatively new. There is not much can go wrong with a refrigerator of major proportions. Many housewives get rid of them simply to get newer models.

I once received a refrigerator sitting outside and apartment at a condominium. I asked the manager what was wrong with it. It was a ten-year-old G.E. Hotpoint and very clean. He said the tenant complained of it iceing up all the time. I took it home and inspected the door gasket. It was hard and cracked in several places. Then I called a Hotpoint dealer and repair shop and found a gasket for it for $35. I hesitated for about a month before deciding to take the chance and repairing it. I replaced the gasket, & cleaned the refrigerator to look like new. I placed an ad and sold it to the first buyer for $135.

Examine every electrical fixture and item you receive. You'll find many stereos, toaster ovens, blenders, etc. thrown into the trash because the cord is defective or the plug needs replaced. Often animals chew through wires and the owners do not think to look for such defects if the items can be replaced for $20 or $30.

FURNITURE. You'll haul away a lot of furniture. Most will truly belong in the dump. But if it's framing is still solid and of good wood, like cherry, maple or oak, and is well constructed, it may be worth renovating.

I was given two upholstered chairs, both torn to shreds by cats' claws and they were very dirty chairs besides. But I knew they were both cherry wood, solid, and originally elegant Queen Anne wing back type chairs. I spent $150 for new upholstery material in a wholesale house, making the material worth twice what I paid, and then I paid $100 to have the chairs recovered and refinished. So for an investment of $250 I had two beautiful chairs. I later sold the pair for $400.

Always take that little extra time to clean up things you plan to sell, especially appliances. People will buy quickly and pay more, if what you have for sale appears to be spotless.

Get books from the library on cleaning and

repairing and restoring. This is time well spent. Eventually you could add hundreds and even thousands to your income.

Read Homer Formby's booklet, <u>Formby's New Guide to Furniture & Home Care.</u> It's filled with tips on cleaning and how to bring life back to old items. It's available free at many hardware and paint stores. Or you can send a self-addressed stamped envelope for a copy to: Homer Formby, P.O. Box 788, Olive Branch, MS. 38654.

TO CLEAN WHITE FURNITURE RINGS. Many common cleaning problems are covered in this helpful booklet. For example, to remove white furniture ring marks left from wet glasses, etc. use a piece of old sheet, t-shirt, or diaper, dampen with water, dab the cloth with toothpaste and buff away the ring. Add baking soda to the toothpaste for stubborn spots.

TO CLEAN METAL. To clean oxidized, uncoated brass, copper or bronze, mix the juice of one lemon with a teaspoon of salt, and apply the mixture to the metal with a piece of fine steel wool. Wet the entire surface, rubbing well with the steel wool. Let it stand for an hour and repeat. Rinse well with water and then dry. Dark spots will appear under the finish if all the salt is not removed when rinsing. Buff to a shine with dry, extra fine steel wool.

TO CLEAN ALUMINUM. To clean exterior painted or unpainted aluminum, mix 50%

motor oil (any weight) with 50% kerosene.
Clean well with this mixture and clean
cloth. Wipe dry and apply a thin coat of
this mixture on the aluminum for future
protection.

I mention this last cleaning procedure for
many aluminum items you might receive. Use
this solution on storm doors still in
usable condition but which have been replaced because they looked so bad.

TO CLEAN PIANO KEYS. To clean piano keys
apply toothpaste to a well dampened cotton
cloth like an old sheet and rub the keys
well. Wipe them dry and buff with a piece
of dry cloth.

Besides tips on furniture finishing,
you'll find ideas on how to clean marble,
vinyl upholstery, leather tops, and the
inside of vases and glass containers with
very small openings.

Things You Can Trade

Trading or bartering is a talent you develop by doing. The more you barter and the
more you read and hear about other people's trading experiences, the better you
become. The magazine MOTHER EARTH NEWS
frequently publishes very good articles on
barter which are worth reading and learning from.

To earn $50 and more an hour, train your-
self to see a use for throw-aways which
others don't think of. Those composted

leaves I mentioned are a useless material to some but for organic gardeners they are essential ingredients for adding nutrition and porosity to their gardens. Offer such loads to your rototilling customers if you offer that service.

TRADE YOUR SERVICES. The first thing you have to trade is your hauling service itself. At $35 per load you know the value of your service. When you run across something you need, or are approached with a proposition to trade, you know the $35 is the unit price you have to work with.

If someone wants to trade an item you don't seem to have a use for, consider it as a possible birthday gift or Christmas gift. Always keep gift giving occasions in mind. You know how heavily your Christmas buying bites into the budget. Nibble away at your Christmas list throughout the year, especially through trade. When Christmas arrives, you can relax and go to your storeroom of gifts and start wrapping.

If you get a call from a dentist or doctor, or need their services, don't hesitate to trade your service for theirs. Tilling a dentists garden for a tooth cleaning or filling is a very convenient trade.

TRADE YOUR HAULING GOODS. When you have a load of apparently useless items which cannot be sold for cash, consider trading. The first trade I made was for 21 wooden screen doors. They were still usable, but were replaced with aluminum storm doors. I took them to a surplus dealer and asked $50 for the lot. The dealer flatly refused and said he wouldn't want them for any price. He said it was close to winter and besides it might take years to sell them all off.

I wasn't discouraged though. Earlier I had seen an upholstered desk chair for $20 and large green slate chalk board for $50 in his inventory. I took them to the dealer and asked if he'd trade even up for the doors. He said no, but for the doors and $10 cash he accepted the deal.

My second trade evolved over a period of months and was simpler than it sounds. I directed the replacement of two oil furnaces in our church and asked the installers to remove the two blower fans and motors from the old furnaces and to set them aside. Heating and air-conditioning contractors usually dump everything - wiring, relays, switches, motors, fans, and furnace shells because they don't have the time to recycle when they are doing many jobs a month. Keep this in mind. A good contract with a heating and air-conditioning contractor could bring you good reusable equipment in exchange for hauling away the debris from his job sites.

I put the fans and motors in my garage and planned to use the best motor for a grinding and sanding machine. At the time I was maintaining an apartment complex for which I needed 2 metal plates to cover a tank in the septic system. I was quoted $50 each at a steel fabricators and decided to wait and find a better price.

On a visit to a surplus store I had the two fans and a blower motor on my truck. I asked the dealer if he'd like to buy them. He said he couldn't use the motor, but he'd consider the fans if the price was right. I said I'd look around to see if there was anything I needed. I found two metal plates the same size and gauge I needed for the septic covers. They were marked $15 each. I offered to trade even up, my two blower fans for his two plates. He accepted.

I then sold the two plates to the apartment complex for $50, or half what they may have paid in the first place. I gave the church $25 and kept the other $25 for my efforts. Later I sold the older of the two motors for $8, and I still have the better of the two.

If you have a repair service consider this idea. Often a customer will have two items for repair, like two vaccuums, or two sewing machines, and he/she does not know if it's worth repairing either one or buying a new one. Offer to repair the best on exchange for the other free. Do this only if the second is worth repairing and you know you can get more for it than the fee you would have charged for repairing the first. You can either sell the renovated machine or use it in another trading deal.

I'd like to repeat: read constantly about other peoples trading experiences. The stories sink into your subconscious, and when you need the information, it will resurface, but in the shape you need for your particular trade. Bartering is not only profitable, but fun.

Things You Can Donate

Clothing, books, and household items you and your family can't use and which are not worth selling will be welcomed by the Salvation Army, Thrift Stores, church bazaars, charities, and special relief programs announced through the news media, or through your childs' school or your church.

Don't limit your donation of books, should you decide not to sell them, to the local library. Your school library needs your help too, maybe more so, as its budget is often much less than public library budgets.

Make it a practice to donate certain portions of your goods. It is wonderful goodwill and helps so many people, and completes the circle you became part of when you were paid to accept these items of value. Getting good usable materials to people who truly need them and cannot afford them is an activity rewarded in ways which cannot be measured.

When you make donations to public organizations, try to remember to ask for a receipt for what you truly think the items are worth. Keep the receipts until tax time. They add up to a good deduction if you make enough donations.

Things You Can Sell As Scrap

SCRAP METAL. Either at home or at your storage facility (a rented garage or barn), unload everything but the heaviest cast iron, tin, or other metals. Sort out all brass, copper, and chrome and throw it into separate five gallon buckets designated for that particular metal.

The wisdom of doing this is best illustrated by my first trip to the salvage yard. I had about 1000 pounds of mixed metals on the truck. I thought it was worth a minimum of $20. I got $8.13. Why? Because I did not separate the metals and thus the dealer estimated the percentages and paid what he wanted to.

Before the next trip I sorted out the brass and copper and took the load to another dealer because I was not comfortable with the first dealers estimate. (It's important to shop around for a dealer you feel you can trust.) This second load was 820 pounds of cast iron and tin, and 19 pounds of brass and copper. I was paid $8.20 for the mixed metals, and $6.46 for the bucket of brass and copper!

So make a habit of throwing all little bits and pieces of brass and copper into a bucket and when it's full take it along with a full load of mixed metals. Ask you dealer how to recognize the most valuable metals. Steel brings higher prices and different grades of steel bring different prices.

Try to schedule your trips to the salvage yard to coincide with other trips to save gas. Take all the metal you can haul safely to the yard. Dealers don't like going through the motions of an entire transaction for a dollars worth of scrap.

MOTOR VEHICLE BATTERIES. Concerning motor vehicle batteries, they are worth $2 to $4 on todays market. Call several dealers and get the best price. Usually scrap yard dealers buy them or will know where you can sell them.

As you can see, the potential profit beyond the initial hauling fee is limited only by your ingenuity and resourcefulness. Stay alert to articles written about recycling. Constantly look for new ways to convert 'junk' back into objects of value and you will soon realize that true wealth is not measured by the number of dollars in your bank account, but by the ideas which generate them. In time, you will see the enormous wealth this nation offers those who simply ask for it (as you will do when you place your ad).

"Will you take this painting worth $400, and here's $35 in cash besides?"

"Being honest is the best thing in the world... it even beats being smart."

9 RECORD KEEPING

The greatest surprise I had waiting from a record-keeping habit I developed as a young boy, was this book and my venture into self-publishing. Had I not kept records, paid taxes, learned how to run a small hauling service, this larger publishing business, which I could not foresee, could not have been possible.

The ability to calculate the average hourly rate from the use of my pick-up was gained solely from my records. Learning to work with an accountant, with bookkeeping systems, were primers for greater things.

An easy form of record keeping for both personal and tax purposes can be accomplished with two books. The first is a simple cash book available in any stationary store. You'd recognize it by it's size, 5-1/2 x 8-1/5. The word CASH is on the cover, and the page format is like the sample shown below. I've added examples of entries and other details.

Sample Journal Entry

Date			Income	Expense	Total
Jan	2	Haul Leonard - Trash	35.		35. 00
"	3	Rent Cutting Torch/Re-til (ABC)		25. 00	10. 00
"	3	Haul Smith - Furnace	70.		80. 00
"	3	Gas - Exxon		10. 00	70. 00

Suggested Bookkeeping System

This is a journal to record earnings on a daily basis. Form a habit of entering amounts daily because you may not remember beyond that and you'll soon find yourself so far behind you'll want to quit keeping the journal. Then you'll have no record of profit or loss and thus no picture to judge your progress or lack of it when reviewing your rate schedule. Nor will you be able to transfer accurate figures to another record book kept monthly for tax purposes.

This second book, available in stationary stores is titled, DOME SIMPLIFIED MONTHLY BOOKKEEPING RECORD by Nicholas Picchione, CPA. It's published by the Dome Publishing Company of Providence, Rhode Island.

It also comes as a Weekly Record, so be sure to make the distinction. This particular book is tan in color and its publication reference is #612.

It's a simple self-explanatory system and you'll soon get to know how to record your earnings and deductions and at the end of the year you simply hand this book over to the accountant or your tax preparer. The price of both of these publications is tax deductible. So is the cost of the accountant and tax preparer.

Read IRS Publication #334 - <u>Tax Guide for a Small Business,</u> available through any IRS office. Knowledge of tax laws will add to your profit, but don't try to be a tax expert. Just familiarize yourself with the deductions which are applicable to your situation.

For example, the cost of your vehicle and its maintenance and repair are deductible. Tools and equipment, the truck rack materials, magazines and publications relating to your business, costs for conversion to a dump truck, and adding a lift gate are deductible. Dumping fees, licenses, insurance, gas mileage while on the job, and that portion of your home you set aside as an office is deductible. So are the heating, furnishings, lighting, phone costs, and answering device deductible.

You'll find a long list of deductions with explanations, so make sure you qualify for them at the front of the DOME BOOKKEEPING RECORD. To further clarify deductions you may never think of, buy or go to the library for a copy of TAKE IT OFF!, by Robert S. Holzman. It is published and updated yearly. Digest as much as you can each year and you'll find over a period of a few years your knowledge can have a tremendous impact on your tax picture.

The value of hiring a CPA for your tax work goes beyond his doing your taxes. The price you pay him to compute your taxes includes occasional consultations throughout the year to answer questions you may have concerning the validity of a deduction. For instance, he can help you with entering certain items into your bookkeeping system, like wages paid to your help.

And because he is working with other small businessmen like yourself who may be in the same situation with regard to how to pay wages, or how best to protect yourself legally with questions such as release of liability he can provide invaluable input which can put your business on a steady upward course. He also has access to current tax information you may not be aware of. The information could save you in a years' time the amount you pay him for that year.

The first year I filed I asked an officer at my bank if he would recommend a good accountant. I approached the accountant and laid all my cards on the able. I simply told him I was new in this business and that I had kept accurate records for the year, had paid no taxes, or Social

Security, or any other kind of taxes. I told him above all I wanted to run an honest business. I asked for his guidance and patience and then left my DOME RECORD BOOK with him.

To my amazement, he informed me later that I had a refund coming in the form of an earned income credit. This refund paid my Federal, State, and Social Security taxes, as well as the accountants' fees. And I had a small amount of cash left over.

So to make it simple in the beginning, keep as accurate a record of your earnings and expenses as you can. Remember to file all receipts for expenses entered as deductions. Don't get bogged down with the details which can take the fun out of running your own business, but don't cheat yourself by not keeping accurate records.

Many times people ask if you want cash instead of a check, thus implying they acknowledge the possibility you may be moonlighting for cash and not reporting the income. This practice, though seeming to be of some immediate advantage, eventually short-circuits itself.

I started this part-time hauling business without any idea where it would take me. My record keeping habit and my moral inclinations would not allow me to ignore my obligation to pay taxes. That first years' experience of receiving a refund after all taxes were paid was incentive enough to continue along the same lines. But then I was reminded by the accountant that my Social Security insurance policy was also being paid.

Though recently there is some question as to the value of the policy, I have received disability payments from Social Security and know what a God-send the payments are when I needed them.

Social Security is not only a retirement insurance. It is also a survivors' insurance which covers your spouse and children in the event of your death. It is Medicare which provides hospital and medical insurance. And of course, it is disability insurance which assures a monthly income if you are unable to work because of illness or other disability.

Once a person has 10 years work credit, he is fully insured for retirement and survivors' benefits, even though he never works again. So for anyone who has been out of the mainstream of the American tax system and is not aware of the side-benefits of paying taxes, running a small business and keeping records and getting earned income credits which pay Social Security, and sometimes kicking back a little besides, it's worth the effort to start considering the advantages of paying taxes.

So when a street corner philosopher tries to convince you that living outside the system is the only way to beat it, consider the source. You usually get such advice from the disenchanted, not from the successful.

One business gives birth to another, and familiarity with the simple mechanics of one small venture will prepare you for even larger endeavors. No job or business is too complex when broken down into its component parts, and each part is performed methodically, and at your own speed and level of present understanding.

Who knows! Take advantage of every opportunity and when you get good enough in a certain area of endeavor to instruct another individual about it and they too succeed with it, sit down and write a report on how to do it. Then start studying about how to sell your report and you're out of blue collar work and into a white collar job of your own making, if thats a direction you'd like to go in.

"When approaching record-keeping, remember the meaning of the word KISS. 'Keep It Simple Stupid'"

"A good attitude and a job well done usually is greeted with the question, 'Do you do anything else?'"

10 RELATED JOB IDEAS

When you go out on a job, keep your eyes open for additional work. You may notice a tree that needs pruning or cutting, a porch which needs repairing, a house which needs painting, or a dilapidated outbuilding which needs to be torn down.

After your job is done and you've been paid, you can chat a bit and in a friendly way say, "Do you need someone to paint your house?" Or, "Do you realize if you tore that old barn down you wouldn't have to pay taxes on it?"

You may discover as I did that $15 an hour hauling jobs develop into $20 an hour contracting jobs in whatever area you find you are good at. Eventually, two-thirds of my yearly gross income came from this unsolicited spin-off business.

Handyman

Often you won't even have to mention other jobs. Many clients ask if you know someone who can do odd jobs. If he asks if you can paint, and it's something you can do, tell him you'll be happy to give him a quote. If it's for painting the exterior of the house, tell him you will get back to him the following day with your bid. As soon as you can, drop by and measure up the job, giving a written quote showing your time estimate and the cost of materials on a standard Job Proposal Form available at stationary stores. I use a form put out by Builders Forms Co., 708 Fayette St., Peoria IL. Ask for form number P811.

It is always best to reduce every activity and material needed for a job into writing so there are no misunderstandings in case there is a delay of weeks, or even months before you get the job or can get to it. It also presents you as a professional, and you protect yourself from the ever-present problem of the client who adds little side jobs to the original job without feeling the need to pay for them.

Spell out exactly what you will be doing for X-number of dollars, and when and how you want to be paid (I always ask for 1/3 to start the job and the balance upon completion). The 1/3 covers the cost of materials, unless the client is providing them, as in the case of supplying the paint to paint his house. If you are doing a fairly long and involved job, ask for the second 1/3 after a few weeks of work has been completed. Then get the balance when you finish. Hold fast to the payment terms as stated on your proposal. The proposal should be signed and dated by you and the client in order to make it legally binding.

This is a legal contract, and you would be softening it's validity if you state you want 1/3 three weeks after the start of the job, or at a certain point in the process of construction, and then do not approach the client and ask for the check on the day it is due.

If you are not careful in such a case, you may find yourself finishing the job without a cent of labor fees and then be given a hard-luck story. Usually you will be asked to accept a small part of what has become a very large balance due to you, and requested to wait until the client can get the rest together.

So, stick to the contract. If you get to that point when payment is due, and anything but a real catastrophe prevents payment, and you do not get the payment, in a very friendly way let the client know you cannot continue the work without the money. Usually everything is so torn up at this stage of the job that you will not have a problem being paid. I mention this aspect of contracting because it does happen every now and then.

If you are asked to do a job you do not know how to do, or don't have time to do, but you know someone who can do it, get that person the job and ask for 10 to 15% commission for the referral.

Get to know a good plumber, electrician, carpenter, and an excavation man. Over a period of a few years the small commissions begin to add up. Make sure the men you recommend are completely reliable and honest. Reputation and credibility are on the line when you make these recommendations.

If you have a natural talent for fixing and figuring things out, and enjoy the diversity of doing odd-jobs, you will never be without work. You can ask $12.50 an hour in most parts of the country and even more in the larger cities. You are a rare and sought after breed if you are honest, sincere, and punctual. You will never have to advertise for work as you are sought after by friends and acquaintances of your satisfied customers.

The quickest way to get into the handyman business is to contact senior citizen groups. Let everyone know you are available for odd-jobs. Once the word gets out and you have completed some jobs, the work will come to you without any effort on your part. Drop into a few real estate agencies and let them know you do odd jobs and exactly what some of them are, or what you are especially good at. Real estate people have a constant supply of jobs which need to be done every time a tenant leaves, or a present tenant calls with a repair complaint.

Remember to set a minimum fee on a repair call, no matter how long the job may take. Charge for a full hour even if the job only takes 15 minutes. Your time to prepare and to get to the job is worth something to you.

If you live in a region where bad winter weather puts a damper on your handyman work, combine that service with a "Fix-it" service at home. Charge your usual hourly rates plus the cost of repair materials. You'll soon know how long each job might take, and if you have to get special parts, tell the customer you'll make a quote later, after you've made calls to your supplier.

Whether as a handyman or a Mr. Fix-it, get to know your suppliers on a personal basis. Tell them you are in business for yourself and you'd like a discount because you will be buying from them on a regular basis. You can usually expect from 10 to 15% off the list price. Don't be shy about asking for this discount. Every supplier expects such requests, and every man in business for himself is getting these price breaks. Charge your customers the full list price. The added advantage of these price breaks is that when buying for your own personal needs, you will be getting the discount.

These price breaks give you a competitive edge on some jobs. For example, I hung an aluminum storm door for a woman who could not pay more than $20.00 for the labor to hang it. I knew it would take three hours.

She knew the price and place to buy the storm door, and that the list price was $110.00. I asked for a contractors price on the door and was given 15% off, or $16.50, and that added to the labor fee of $20.00 gave me $36.50. The discount made it worth my time to take the job.

The best advice in this and any service job is to never stop reading and learning how to do more and more types of jobs. And be willing to share your knowledge. Helping a client to save money by explaining how to change his own faucet washers will be returned a hundred-fold when you are the first to come to mind when jobs too difficult and time consuming come up for the client.

Grounds Work

Grounds work is the extra work which will come most frequently. Leaf raking, grass cutting, brush clearing, and gutter cleaning(house roof gutters) always need doing. If you haven't done this kind of work before, take on the jobs by yourself at first and get familiar with the machinery and various tools of the trade. Then when you can demonstrate a good well-manicured look for a clients property, take on a helper and teach him what you learned. A simple rule for earning more is "Don't divide yourself, multiply yourself."

When working up rates for this service, ask other lawn care operators what they charge. If you have to, invite a few operators over to your property, or your parents property and ask how much they'd charge to have the grass cut and trimmed once a week. While talking, mention you might sometime like to have the hedge trimmed, or a tree pruned. Down the line when some young fellow wants to create a business for himself, don't forget to share the same information with him.

After getting the other operators' quotes, divide their quoted figures by the number of hours you estimate your job will take. This is your hourly rate. Subtract your helpers wage from this figure and you have your own profit for the hour.

I'll pass along some experience concerning the wage you pay your help in grounds work or any work for that matter. This is hard work, and usually is done in the heat of the day. And the bugs don't make it any more pleasant. If you pay your help minimum wage, expect to get minimum effort and minimum attention to detail.

Its better to pay more to a young man who is conscientious and wants to do a good job than try to earn a bit more by taking on a man who is willing to accept the minimum wage. It's well worth a smaller profit to have a contented reliable man on the job.

When a man feels his efforts are appreciated, not only through compliments but by above average wages, he will respond accordingly. You'll find that man on the job before you, he'll not leave you high and dry at the most crucial moments, and he won't tend to disappear for a few days each time he gets his pay check.

Tree Service

Pruning and falling trees is not an exact science, but a little study at the library and talking to some old-timers about it would help. Start by accepting small tree jobs, trimming hedges and bushes, and get good at these. Then work your way up to more difficult jobs like falling trees 20' to 30' high. Never cut a tree down without attaching a rope to it somewhere up near the top. Have a second man direct the tree to where you want it to fall. Unless of course, you are in the middle of a field or are in the woods and it doesn't matter which way it goes.

Maybe a seasoned woodsman would laugh at this precaution. But my brother had a professional tree faller help him drop a huge tree on his property without the aid of a guide rope. The cut seemed just right, the lean was right, everything seemed favorable. Still the tree turned on the stump and fell on my brothers brand new greenhouse.

Ask around for what men are charging for different sized trees.

Make certain for a business like this you have a large, heavy-duty, well running chainsaw. Carry at least two reserve chains, and possibly a smaller back-up chainsaw.

You can charge from $200 a day to cut unspecified numbers of trees on one property. People living on hillsides often find their prized views begin to disappear after a good many years of tree growth. They call a tree service to either top the offending trees, or drop the worst violators.

My first big job was for $250 for a day of cutting. I agreed to use the clients saw because mine was in repair. I'd never do that again! The chain was dull, the saw would not start, and when it did it would not keep running. After numerous attempts to get it running, I had to excuse myself and take it in for prompt repair. The quick fix did not work and I lost a half a day before I rented a good machine and soon had the customer smiling. She thought the trouble was with me and not her saw. The lesson was well learned.

Consider buying a pair of tree climbers which attach to the side of the ankles. In areas where there are palm trees, people have the dead palm branches trimmed from the underside. These ankle spikes are ideal for such work. They're also good for topping trees.

One good advantage to tree falling is the possibility of the tree being suitable for firewood which you can later sell for another profit.

Cut hardwood in the spring and early summer and let it dry until the following winter. Sell it then for a premium as cured firewood. Run one ad for your tree service and another one for customers to buy firewood by the cord. Take orders all year long and deliver when the wood is cured and the customers have the need. You can tell people who have fireplaces you would like to put them on your list for the following winter.

A man I know offers to cut trees down for nothing provided there are enough hardwoods to make it worth his time. Many property owners have a wood lot close to their homes and want it thinned. These owners get a job done they cannot ordinarily afford, and it's done for nothing in exchange for the hardwood.

Cutting and selling firewood is a first cousin business to a tree service. Visit lumber mills. Many operate for supplying specialized markets. For instance, one I know of cuts only ash trees which are cut to a basic square shape and sent to another mill where baseball bats are produced. For $15 per truckload, anyone could buy slabs and leftovers from the mill operations. A half-ton pick-up can carry about 1/2 cord of green hardwood. A cord of ash kindling from this mill therefore cost $30.00.

Watch for new mills as they can spring up over night. One mill opened near us to cut wood for cedar shakes and it had a good bit of small kindling sized leftovers. A truckload was going for $15. A bundle of that same kindling, only a few pounds worth, was selling for $1.00 in the local supermarket. Think about bundling and supplying your own local market.

In some areas of the country a free permit can be obtained for cutting a specific number of cords of wood from specified areas within government land. Call the state forest department, or the Department of the Interior. Someone in either of these agencies will lead you to the agency providing the permit and information about quantity allowed and areas for cutting.

Snow Removal

You can find jobs snow-shovelling and plowing. Contact condominiums, and apartment complexes and advertise to build a list of regular residential customers.

Charge a minimum fee ($15 for example, no matter how short a time it takes to clear all the agreed upon areas.) Seven dollars an hour is reasonable to arrive on your own and make certain the walks and steps are cleared before anyone gets out to work. Work out the specific details with the managers and have it in writing so there are no misunderstandings once the snow begins to fall. Ask how deep the snow must be for you to arrive for the job. Often it will be left to your discretion.

If you have a plow, take a young helper along to shovel while you do the plowing.

Charge by the job when plowing and providing a shoveller.

Rototilling Service

If you own or can rent a good rototiller, you can ask for $20 an hour minimum. And ask for no less. Any questions about the rate and I suggest the customer try hand turning the garden to a foots depth and have it as fine as coffee grains. Or offer to hand turn it yourself for $5.00 per hour. Let him know it will take all day and maybe more. Of course you are not serious, but it should get your point across.

Rototilling Ad Sample

Build a customer list by placing the following ad:

```
ROTO-TILLING.   Call now for your appoint-
ment.   555-1212.
```

Notice this time I do not state the price. I prefer quoting the $20 an hour figure on the phone so any questions can be answered while I have the prospect on the line. I don't want to lose a client even before I get a chance at his business. I used a Troy-bilt roto-tiller and many customers who knew gardening seldom questioned my rates after hearing what machine I had.

This is such a good side-line business to hauling that I'm including the following information for you to use to get further details. Write to: TROY-BILT Roto Tillers, 102nd & 9th Av., Troy, N.Y. 12180. Tell them you want to go into business.

Call your tilling customers in the spring and fall. Not all will want fall tilling, but many do. Ask your customers for referrals. You can often get hauling and fix-it jobs from your tilling customers too.

Don't forget condos and apartments provide garden plots for the owners and tenants. Mention it to the managers that you have a tilling service and ask him to pass your name around. Or print a small ad and place it in a conspicuous place, like in the laundry room or under peoples' doors.

The rental fees or cost of a new or used roto-tiller, lawn equipment, etc., are all tax deductible.

High Pressure Cleaning Service

You can rent an air compressor with long hoses attached to a wand and gun-type handle similar to the kind used in car washes. After you earn enough, buy the compressor and find where you can get the special attachments for cleaning all kinds of things.

For example, every spring a couple of men arrive at a friends trailer park and knock on doors offering to wash the exterior of the trailer from top to bottom. They charge $40 and up depending on the size and difficulty of the job. A soap solution is added to the set-up to dispense under high pressure, just like a car wash. The compressor sits on their pickup and hoses are connected to the customers water supply. The average job takes about an hour and a half.

Members of my church washed our entire church, top to bottom, our storage shed, and the lower floor of another building on the grounds. It took six hours. The white aluminum siding had become dirty and brown from road dust and many corners and crevices were full of spider webs to which leaves and other debris became attached. Our first attempt at hand washing got as far as one wall on the front porch before we gave up and rented a pressure washer.

Approach churches and public building managers for their business. Charge by the hour or by the job, starting at about $15 an hour and work your way into higher fees as you get the feel of how long a job takes and how much you can charge in your area.

Consider contracting with the phone company to spray clean their public phone booths. Don't think these contracts are out of reach until you have tried. Call the main office and be persistent about getting the right person to discuss your proposal.

The bus companies also contract to have

their bus-stops cleaned periodically. A fellow I met travels around in his van cleaning busses for the bus company, beer trucks for the distributors, and delivery trucks for Pepsi-Cola and Coca-Cola. You'd think they would have their own facilities, but apparently it's more cost effective to farm the work out than buy the equipment and hire a man to do the job.

Buy your cleaning materials wholesale.

You may be surprised to find no one is operating a portable high pressure cleaning service in your area and thus have the advantage of setting your rates as the market will bear them. Develop a rate card for standard jobs like trailer cleaning, building cleaning, etc. This standard quoting system assures a businesslike approach and prevents your having to haggle and dicker with each new customer.

Ask at the rental firm for the many uses of the high pressure machine. I stripped a large piece of cedar driftwood of all its bark and other unwanted loose material in preparation for turning it into a base for a coffee table. The sprayer performs like a sand blasting device but is less damaging. Though, beware. If you get too close to soft wood it will pit the surface. And by all means be careful not to direct the spray at any part of your own body or anyone elses. The pressure is strong enough to penetrate the skin or even blow a hole in it.

You can blast loose paint from a house or furniture or machinery in preparation for painting. You can clean car and truck engines and undercarriages of road salt and tar. The list is endless. Put together a flyer describing all these features and spread it around.

Demolition And Salvage

On some jobs, especially in rural areas, you may notice a run-down building - an old garage, barn or other out-building - on the premises. Offer to tear it down. Because conventional demolition companies charge fairly high prices, many landowners leave these old buildings standing and thus pay taxes on them year after year.

Determine what demolition companies are charging to tear properties down in your area. Contact construction companies and ask for their demoliton work when it comes to them. Let the contractor know you are willing to do better in price than other local firms because you work alone or with only one helper. But also set a minimum for which you will work. As a guideline, a two-car garage should bring about $300.00. Of course, a house of the same size would have more interior structure to remove, and thus would bring more. Don't tear buildings down for the salvage value of the materials alone, which is what many people would like you to do. Charge for your labor. You don't know if what you get will be worth your time in tearing it down, or if you will have the opportunity to convert the salvage into cash.

You can advertise for business too. And check with your town or city clerk for licenses or fees applicable to demolition. Ask about permits for tearing the buildings down. The client should pay for this permit, but if not include its cost in the the contract.

As in any constructionwork, put your proposal in writing and go over it with the client so after you're finished, you do not find it was understood you were to fill in the basement under the structure. At first, don't offer to do this part of a demolition job. Have the client hire an independent bull-dozer operator, or if you know how to operate one, rent it and include the rental price in the contract.

Demolition work requires a storage area and an interior space to sort and clean salvageable materials. If the building is mostly rotten and of no value for salvage, don't work with small tools. I mean, cut the building down with a chain saw. You can have a medium-sized building on the ground in one day. It may cost you a chain or two but the same work done with a sledge and crow bar could take days.

If the building does have good salvageable material, dismantle it carefully in reverse of how it was built. Remove everything from the interior first - loose debris strewn around, furniture, junk, etc. Then carefully remove the windows. Take off interior moldings, electrical and plumbling fixtures, and any good wood flooring. Then take down the walls.

Move outside to the roof and take off the shingles, or whatever roof covering there is, then the board or sheathing underneath, and then the framing. If there's a chimney, start taking it apart as gently as you can if it's made of bricks. You can resell them for 15 to 20 cents each after you clean off the mortar. Dismantle the chimney down to the roof line.

Take off the exterior walls and deconstruct the rest of the frame. The remainder of the chimney could be taken down as you work with the wall framing.

Load what you tear away as you go along, and haul it back to your storage area or to the dump. That way no huge piles of rubble form and it's much easier to classify the materials as you go along. It will also present an orderly worksight.

Sort and remove the nails from all your materials and classify everything according to size. Keep a list as you go along so that at any given time if you have an offer for a piece or a whole load, you can quickly come up with a price.

To price your materials, get the prices of new materials of the same size and wood type, and the used price from other dealers who sell used wood. Hand-hewn beams are worth a lot more then ordinary used lumber and should be given a premium price. Your ordinary used lumber should bring about half the price as new lumber. Check the prices other demolition companies are charging for their used lumber.

The demand for old well-seasoned wood is high, especially for barn boards, and rough hand-hewn timbers. An ad in your local paper, or one in larger city paper close to your home will bring people out on the weekends. Don't forget you run a hauling business, so don't offer free delivery unless you need to put some grease on a slow moving transaction for a large deal.

For more complete details on this subject, and how to charge for demolition labor, salvage materials, and other aspects of the business, read the following informative articles. Both can be located at your library or back issues may be bought from the publisher.

THE MOTHER EARTH NEWS, "Success with Demolition & Salvage", issue #70, July-August, 1981. Page 79.

THE MOTHER EARTH NEWS, "Booming Barn-Board Business", issue #67, January-February, 1981. Page 22.

Scavenging

You may or may not like to scavenge, but it can be very rewarding. Scavenging, as I use the term is examining goods and materials for their further utility. It does not mean going through organic garbage and refuse. Public dumps are usually divided into sections. And the organic garbage goes into one area. Non-organic matter, like construction material, furniture, clothes, appliances, paper goods, etc., go into another area. It is to this area you will take most of your loads. And in this area it is smart to keep alert to what has been thrown away.

Some town dumps allow scavenging. That is, they allow you to take away what you can use. Periodically check through construction materials, or bags and boxes. You will many times find car batteries thrown into the dump. At $2 to $4 each they are good finds. You never know what lies under what looks like useless goods.

If you live in or near a city, cruise the streets in the early morning hours, especially in the higher rent districts. It will surprise you what wealthier people will consider to be throw-away items. There is a wealth of construction materials, furniture, and small and large repairable appliances deposited on the streets daily. This aspect of scavenging alone could keep you busy on a permanent basis.

Set up a system for picking up goods on ona day, and reselling them on another. Or have a partner make the pick-ups and you sell or vice-versa.

I know a theater group which had no capital for its sets and scenery or other materials like costumes. In a six month period they filled a 40 foot x 80 foot loft with everything they needed. They found seats, real lamp posts, fireplace fronts, stair rails, wooden pillars, gargoyles, drapery material, costume material, tables and chairs, sofas, lamps, beds, and all of it came from the streets.

I relate this story because I envision a man who is building a second home or summer cottage in the suburbs, coming into the city on a weekly basis supplying many needs he may never be able to afford. Foresight is a real virtue. So, if you have a house building project in your future, you should begin collecting the things you will need way in advance.

I saw a story on PM MAGAZINE about a man who took a large magnet to tract home developments after work hours and scanned the areas around new carpentry activities. He gathered up enough nails to supply his entire week-end summer home building project. This may seem like a lot of work and time lost for apparently small ticket items, but this same man, who also collected many other materials in very innovative fashions, plans to move into his home mortgage free.

He saw the wisdom of exchanging this time for his lack of future indebtedness.

Watch the newspapers for the times and places of seasonal town and city clean-up campaigns. Again, it's smart to concentrate on the upper-income areas.

Always keep alert to ways of creating business where it does not appear to be. Scavenging for slightly damaged materials and hiring repairmen to make them saleable is creating business. Work in conjunction with a flea marketeer, consignment shop or run a perpetual garage sale, or open a shop of your own.

The rewards of such innovative thinking go far beyond the immediate cash profit. The fabric of our economy is strengthened. Ben Franklin's statement, "Waste not, want not," is provable, even today.

Delivery Service

If you own a van, you might consider a delivery service. Depending on what you deliver, your rates should start at about $25 an hour. In New York City the going rate is about $36 an hour.

Specializing your service, such as delivering only objects of art and antiques can demand more as you must carry insurance to protect yourself, though the owners of the art or antiques and the dealers also carry insurance for any losses incurred during transit. One young man I know delivered a piece of sculpture to Erie, Pa. from New York City and was paid $900.00, or roughly $1 a mile out and back. And he completed the job in a day and a half. It was a high price to pay, but the sculptors' piece got the personal attention the artist demanded.

A delivery service of any kind is in great demand in the larger cities, and is well worth considering. The same rule applies for developing a rate schedule. When you get a call from an ad, tell the prospect you will get back to him. Then call a few competitors and ask what they would charge for such a job, then call your prospect and give your price. When I tell you to call your competitors, remember, you are to act as though you are requiring their services. Don't tell them you are in the delivery service too.

Consider combining a hauling business and a delivery service to keep your schedule full. Run ads for both businesses and see which you prefer or which brings the most profit. Again, read other delivery service ads and adapt one to your own needs.

Contact large appliance stores, especially individually owned businesses. Ask the manager if he needs a free-lance delivery man. Work out a delivery fee in terms of load size and mileage. Use the chart in the center of the book for mileage rates. Even stores as large as Sears hires independent delivery men. In the East, the delivery trucks operating for Sears are trucks owned independently but they're painted the Sears colors and bear the Sears logo.

Lumber yards and building centers make small deliveries. Approach them in the same way and leave your rate card. If you talk with the managers of these centers, they know what is fair to charge and would thus help to put your rate chart together.

Another aspect of a delivery service which can be rewarding is contracting with the publishers of Pennysavers, Shoppers Guides, etc., the free publications found in supermarkets, drugstores, and other outlets. Approach the publishers and ask for their delivery business.

This business is like a glorified paper boys job. But then so are the rewards. Starting with one truck and working up to four trucks, a man in Phoenix, Arizona is grossing $52,000 a year doing just this. He says he can't handle all the business offered to him. Even larger newspapers sub-contract their delivery work.

Sharpening Service

Approach a local sharpening service and suggest you become his outside man. Many times business and home owners would be better served if they did not have to take scissors or mower blades to the shop. Or they simply never have the sharpening done. They buy new implements instead.

I was in a shop in Princeton, New Jersey and noticed a man in a van pull up and walk from shop to shop asking to sharpen any knives and scissors on the premises. He charged $2 a pair for scissors and took about five minutes. He also had a key duplicating service on the back of the van. Anyone needing another apartment key had this Johnny-on-the-spot do it for him.

His van was painted with his portable advertisement. He said his best accounts were restaurants whom he called only regularly for sharpening their chefs knives.

Pest Control Service

Go to work for a pest control business. Find out what equipment is needed and then when you are familiar with the different chemicals and how to use them, find where you can get the equipment to set up your own business. Most of the neighborhoods near us are serviced by independents who work either out of their pick-ups or vans.

Pilot Vehicle

That pick-up you see with the two flashing yellow lights on its roof driving out in front of a trailer which is pulling half a section of a double-wide home is usually an independent driver. Call trailer sales companies, or better yet, stop in and tell them you are interested in such jobs. Ask if they are hiring independents for this kind of job. If not, ask them for recommendations. Get leads until you finally have a solid offer for work. Otherwise, at least get your name placed on file for future work or to fill in if their is a no-show.

You'll need a CB and a set of flashing yellow lights for the top of your cab. Buy both second-hand if you can. The fees for such jobs start at about 80 cents a mile. It's a slow ride to your destination, but it beats heavy labor at minimum wages.

These examples of spin-off businesses from the hauling jobs I've shown you how to get can eventually put you into a lifetime occupation. They aren't far-flung ideas, beyond the grasp of most individuals. My intention is to let anyone who owns a pick-up or van know that no matter where he or she might find himself, his source of employment is right there with him. A pick-up or van, a small ad and this book, and you're the head of your own company, anytime, anywhere.

And now, "Gentlemen, start your engines!"

APPENDIX

Release of Liability Sample

I, (helper's name), agree that I am responsible for my own taxes on wages paid by (your name), and I will not hold (your name) liable for any injuries I might suffer while in the performance of work for (your name).

Date:_____   Signature:(helper's name)

Make copies of the following form and have it signed before you take a new helper on any job.

Release of Liability Form

I, _____ agree that I am

responsible for my own taxes on wages paid

by _____, and I will not

hold _____ liable for any

injuries I might suffer while in the per-

formance of work for _____.

Date:_____   Signature:_____.

me & my

AT YOUR SERVICE

555-1234
Your Name

General Hauling * Light Moving * Odd Jobs

HAVE TRUCK ~ WILL HAUL

Your Name   Telephone
General Hauling * Light Moving * Odd Jobs
Trash Removal * Construction Clean-up

Call: Name/Telephone

General Hauling * Light Moving * Odd Jobs
Trash Removal * Construction Clean-up

Your Name   Telephone

Sample Business Cards/Layout for Printer

me & my

AT YOUR SERVICE

HAVE TRUCK ~ WILL HAUL

Use this artwork for your business cards and fill in your own information. Have your printer enlarge the artwork 133% for use on business cards.

Artwork For Master Section

me & my

.AT YOUR SERVICE

Make a copy of this artwork at your copy center. At home, divide up an 8-1/2x11 sheet of paper into 8 sections. Measure one section and that will be the size of your square to type in your own details, after you have pasted the artwork at the top of the square. Again go to your copy center, make 8 copies of your master section, paste them into the 8 blank sections on your 8-1/2x11 paper. This is now your final master copy. Keep it clean and in a safe place. Copy it over and over for 8 ads each.

Sample Display Ad Master Section

me & my

.AT YOUR SERVICE

HAULING
TRASH REMOVAL
CONSTRUCTION CLEAN-UP
ODD JOBS
LIGHT MOVING

Reasonable Rates

Don Lilly
555-1234

Sample Display Ad Master Copy

me & my 🚛 *AT YOUR SERVICE*

HAULING
TRASH REMOVAL
CONSTRUCTION CLEAN-UP
ODD JOBS
LIGHT MOVING

Reasonable Rates
Don Lilly
555-1234

me & my 🚛 *AT YOUR SERVICE*

HAULING
TRASH REMOVAL
CONSTRUCTION CLEAN-UP
ODD JOBS
LIGHT MOVING

Reasonable Rates
Don Lilly
555-1234

me & my 🚛 *AT YOUR SERVICE*

HAULING
TRASH REMOVAL
CONSTRUCTION CLEAN-UP
ODD JOBS
LIGHT MOVING

Reasonable Rates
Don Lilly
555-1234

me & my 🚛 *AT YOUR SERVICE*

HAULING
TRASH REMOVAL
CONSTRUCTION CLEAN-UP
ODD JOBS
LIGHT MOVING

Reasonable Rates
Don Lilly
555-1234

me & my 🚛 *AT YOUR SERVICE*

HAULING
TRASH REMOVAL
CONSTRUCTION CLEAN-UP
ODD JOBS
LIGHT MOVING

Reasonable Rates
Don Lilly
555-1234

me & my 🚛 *AT YOUR SERVICE*

HAULING
TRASH REMOVAL
CONSTRUCTION CLEAN-UP
ODD JOBS
LIGHT MOVING

Reasonable Rates
Don Lilly
555-1234

me & my 🚛 *AT YOUR SERVICE*

HAULING
TRASH REMOVAL
CONSTRUCTION CLEAN-UP
ODD JOBS
LIGHT MOVING

Reasonable Rates
Don Lilly
555-1234

me & my 🚛 *AT YOUR SERVICE*

HAULING
TRASH REMOVAL
CONSTRUCTION CLEAN-UP
ODD JOBS
LIGHT MOVING

Reasonable Rates
Don Lilly
555-1234

Enlarge this page to the preferred size at a copy center. If the ad in my sample suits your needs, type your name and phone number on a piece of paper, cut it out and paste it over mine in each block. Then copy that new master sheet over and over again. Refer for further details to page 35.

SPECIAL GIFT OFFER

The author, Don Lilly, will send you a special personally autographed gift copy of this book in return for a signed and dated notarized copy of a story or stories, with or without photos, of your most incredible job, 'find', or treasure, and the amount you were paid to do the job, or take the treasure away. Your story may be used for future publicity or mention in future editions of this book, but only your initials and city or town will be printed. Send this page with your story. Sign and date it as an authorization for use of your materials with no further remuneration than the gift copy.

We'd like to hear how hauling has supported families between jobs, supplemented incomes, etc. If you like, tell us about yourself, your profession, what you drive, why you love your pick-up. We know there are fantastic stories out there. If you use your pick-up to make money in an unusual way, tell us about that too. We'll possibly share it with our readers in the next edition. Sign & date this form and return it with your notarized story.

Signature_____

Date_____

Send to: **DARIAN BOOKS** P.O. Box 3091, Glendale, AZ 85311

Pickup Truck Dump Box

ATTENTION PICKUP OWNER

Would you like to have a load dumping capability for your truck without spending $1000-$1500 for a conventional hydraulic system???????

With less than $150 worth of materials, you can build and install this Pickup Truck Dump Box in your truck in one weekend . . . . . .

Detailed step-by-step Instruction Booklet for fabrication, installation, and operation in any size/style pickup bed is NOW AVAILABLE for $10.00.

Judged "Best New Invention" at the SPRING '83 NEW PRODUCTS AND INVENTIONS EXPO, *Nashville, Tn., Apr. 1, 2, 3, 1983.*

U.S. Letters Patent Applied For—Currently Pending.

Use order provided on pages 126 and 128.

Free information available

FLEA MARKET HANDBOOK

BY ROBERT G. MINER

WARNING: This Book Could Make You Rich!

Flea Market Handbook is about turning the "junque" around your home into an original investment in the antiques field. Step-by-step the author shows how, without cash you can set up a business in a nearby flea market and make your collection grow into a small fortune.

All the tricks of the trade are covered - how to set up - how to deal with cranky customers - how to turn hagglers into buyers - how to buy right from auctions and homes - how to price your merchandise - how to keep necessary records - how to build an expanding, satisfying business.

Hundreds of thousands of shoppers, perhaps millions, attend flea markets every weekend. Here's your guide to getting into the market.

156 pages $9.95

Use order provided on pages 126 & 128. If no order blanks, send $9.95 + $1.00 postage and handling to:

DARIAN·BOOKS

P.O. Box 3091
Glendale, AZ 85311
(602) 931-3788

ORDER FORM

Please send me the following:

_____copies of How To Earn $15 To $50
An Hour & More With A Pick-up Truck Or
Van   by Don Lilly $12.95@

_____copies of Flea Market Handbook
by Robert G. Miner $9.95@

_____copies of Pick-up Truck Dump Box
Instruction Booklet $10.00@

I understand I may return books or booklet
for a full refund if not satisfied.

Name_____

Address_____

_____Zip_____

Arizona Residents: Add 6 1/2% sales tax. (.65
cents)

Shipping: $1 for the first book and .25 cents
for each additional book.

_____3 to 4 weeks is too long. Here is $2.50
per book for FIRST CLASS.

(DARIAN·BOOKS)
P.O. Box 3091
Glendale, AZ 85311
(602)931-3788

ORDER FORM

Please send me the following:

_____copies of How To Earn $15 To $50
An Hour & More With A Pick-up Truck Or
Van   by Don Lilly $12.95@

_____copies of Flea Market Handbook
by Robert G. Miner $9.95@

_____copies of Pick-up Truck Dump Box
Instruction Booklet $10.00@

I understand I may return books or booklet
for a full refund if not satisfied.

Name_____

Address_____

_____Zip_____

Arizona Residents: Add 6 1/2% sales tax. (.65
cents)

Shipping: $1 for the first book and .25 cents
for each additional book.

_____3 to 4 weeks is too long. Here is $2.50
per book for FIRST CLASS.

⟨ DARIAN·BOOKS ⟩

P.O. Box 3091
Glendale, AZ 85311
(602)931-3788